A TIME TO LIVE

The case against euthanasia
and assisted suicide

George Pitcher

MONARCH
BOOKS

Oxford, UK, & Grand Rapids, Michigan, USA

First published in the UK in 2010 by Monarch Books
(a publishing imprint of Lion Hudson plc)
Wilkinson House, Jordan Hill Road, Oxford OX2 8DR, England
Tel: +44 (0)1865 302750 Fax: +44 (0)1865 302757
Email: monarch@lionhudson.com
www.lionhudson.com

ISBN 978 1 85424 987 6

Distributed by:
UK: Marston Book Services, PO Box 269, Abingdon, Oxon, OX14 4YN

Scripture quotations are from the New Revised Standard Version published by HarperCollins Publishers, copyright © 1989 by the Division of Christian Education of the National Council of the Churches of Christ in the USA, and are used by permission. All rights reserved.

The text paper used in this book has been made from wood independently certified as having come from sustainable forests.

British Library Cataloguing Data
A catalogue record for this book is available from the British Library.

Printed and bound in the UK by MPG Books.

£8.99

A TIME TO LIVE

To our uncle, Captain Brian Brownscombe GM, Regimental
Medical Officer, 2nd Battalion The South Staffordshire
Regiment (Airborne), who died at Arnhem on 24th September
1944, offering others all that he was denied

CONTENTS

ACKNOWLEDGMENTS

I have very many people to thank for help and inspiration with this book: Tony Collins, whose idea it was, and his team at Monarch; Professor Paul Badham, whose own book on the subject I disagreed with so profoundly that I agreed to write this one; all colleagues at the Telegraph for quiet encouragement. In the medical field, Ilora Finlay at the House of Lords and her various good offices have been more than an education and I owe her a huge debt. Also Dr Nicholas Ramscar, whose testimony I use, and Jullien Gaer, of Harefield Hospital, who explained life and death over claret. I also have another parliamentary contact to thank, without whom I would not have been able to complete the project, but who wishes to remain anonymous – you know who you are and I tip my hat. Profound thanks for the thought leadership of Archbishops Rowan Williams and Vincent Nichols. All these people shared their professional expertise and the intelligence included in this book is theirs, any errors mine. Finally, loving thanks to Mum, Dad and Auntie Anne, who showed me what it means to share the whole journey.

FOREWORD

Should we legalise assisted suicide or euthanasia? That is a question that has come to front of the political stage in the last few years. It is certainly an important one. As medical science has advanced, we have begun to live longer and to become more susceptible to malignant or degenerative illnesses. Some believe that doctors should do more than treat our illnesses and relieve our pain and distress – they should, it is being suggested, be licensed to put us down or help us to kill ourselves, if that is what we say we want. This new agenda comes in sheep's clothing. Euphemisms, such as "assisted dying" or "end of life assistance" all disguise the reality of deliberately ending life months or years early. The propaganda is full of words like "dignity", "compassion" and "choice". And, in case we still harbour reservations, we are told not to worry as there would be "safeguards".

The trouble is that, when you look beneath the surface, you see that it isn't as simple as the propagandists would have us believe. This topic is a highly complex ethical, legal, clinical and social issue. The more each strand of the debate is examined, the more evident it becomes that the picture the euthanasia lobby paints is a distorted one. It's not true, for example, that the law we have is cruel and unreasonable or that seriously ill people are dying in pain all over the country or that "assisted dying" is working well in the few countries where it has been legalised. As a palliative care physician, I have looked after thousands of patients over the last 23 years as their lives drew to a close. I cannot claim that every one of them has died without distress – no one could ever say that. But I do know that "bad deaths" these days are much rarer than when I was a young doctor in the 1970s. Then we just did not know what to do, pain and distress in dying were commonplace and were just accepted as the norm.

In the same way, if you look no further than media stories, you could be forgiven for thinking that there is a rush of seriously ill people to Switzerland to end their lives in the death apartment run by the ill-named Dignitas. This just isn't so. Over the last 10 years around one in every 50,000 British deaths has taken place this way and many were not terminally ill at all. Such deaths are news precisely because they are rare.

Let me be clear. I do not question the intentions or integrity of those who want to see the law changed. I question their realism. Their proposals to legalise "assisted dying" assume the existence of a perfect world - a world in which all doctors know their patients well enough to understand their underlying fears and anxieties and to assess whether a request for euthanasia stems from firm conviction, rather than from a sense of hopelessness or obligation to others. They assume a world in which all terminally ill people know their own minds clearly, are never vulnerable to any pressures, never have depressed thinking that has gone undiagnosed and that the information they have about their prognosis and future is always completely accurate. Anyone who works, day in and day out, with dying people knows that this idealised picture simply does not reflect reality.

This is why the appearance of George Pitcher's book is such a timely and helpful contribution to the debate. He charts accurately the rise of the individualistic culture that lies at the root of calls for "assisted dying" and he exposes eloquently the reality rather than the spin of what has been happening in the American State of Oregon, so beloved of British would-be reformers, as well as Holland. He then proceeds to give a much-needed exposition of how euthanasia law has developed and how it works in Britain today, concluding with the revised prosecution policy that has recently appeared from the Crown Prosecution Service – a policy whose robustness must have come as a serious disappointment to the euthanasia lobby.

Mr Pitcher then turns to the medical scene, rebutting the facile argument that, if we can put down our pets when they are ill, we should do the same for our fellow humans. He exposes the intriguing paradox that campaigning for euthanasia and assisted suicide has increased almost in parallel with modern medicine's ability to relieve suffering and questions why "assisted dying", if it ever were to be legalised, has to be part of health care.

It is an excellent book and I hope it will be widely read by everyone who has an interest in this subject.

Professor the Baroness Finlay of Llandaff FRCP, FRCGP.

INTRODUCTION

I tried to kill my mother in 1993. I didn't attempt the act myself, you understand, but I asked a nurse to increase her morphine dosage to a lethal level, so that she might be washed away on an opiate tide. At seventy-five, Mum had been operated on for a brain tumour, but the cancer had spread uncontrollably and they had stitched her up and told us she hadn't got long left. My sister made her comfortable in her house, and when her condition nosedived, I took the train to the West Country and found my sister taking a break in the garden. It was easy to see why. Mum was unconscious, but taking great, rattling last gasps of breath, her body clearly staging one last, hopeless rage against the dark.

When the nurse came that afternoon to change her morphine drip, I begged her, in tears, to bring this pointless suffering to an end. The nurse was lovely: patient and kind, but firm. No, she said, she couldn't do that, but she held my hand and said that all would be well soon. Given all the fuss recently about nurses offering prayer for their patients, I recall that she also assured me that Mum would be "better" soon. It was an act of excellent and professional pastoral care.

She was right, of course – about the morphine dosage, I mean. That evening, the morphine faded and Mum regained consciousness for a few minutes. We could talk to her, hold her, say goodbye, tell her we loved her. She couldn't speak, but she struggled to communicate with my sister and me, with her eyes and her smile. And I realized in awe that, in a final, selfless act of motherhood, she was comforting us, rather than the other way round.

I wouldn't have missed that last exchange for the world and, of course, I will carry it with me, as a comfort and a revelation of the meaning of death, for the rest of my own life. But had the nurse been able to respond to my earlier pleas for release, we would have been denied those precious fifteen minutes. I shiver when I think of what I could have lost, had a medical professional not saved me from myself.

It's always dangerous to extrapolate the personal to the general, but the experience has partly forged my passionate opposition to assisted suicide, which Lord Falconer, the former Lord Chancellor and Justice Secretary, like Lord Joffe before him, has attempted and failed to have legalized in the House of Lords. They and other supporters of the introduction of assisted suicide in Britain would stress that their campaign has nothing to do with the circumstances of our family and my mother, because they are not advocating euthanasia; so, had my initial pleas been answered, the nurse and I would still have rightly faced criminal charges under their proposals.

But that is disingenuous of them. The assisted-suicide lobbying group Dignity in Dying declares that its mission is "the option of an assisted death for terminally ill, mentally competent adults". My mother was terminally ill. I've no doubt that, at an earlier stage, she would have requested a convenient exit if she thought it would protect us. Furthermore, those campaigning for assisted suicide won clarification from the Director of Public Prosecutions in 2010 over the circumstances under which someone assisting a suicide might escape prosecution. In delivering his guidance, the DPP shifted his focus of the drafting stage from the circumstances of the person asking for an assisted suicide to the motives of those doing the assisting. One of the factors that would militate against prosecution would be if the assistant to a suicide acted out of "compassion". I'm satisfied that when I implored the nurse to end my mother's life, I was acting with all the loving compassion that everyone talks about when they take their loved ones to death clinics such as Dignitas in Switzerland. So they may deny it, but the assisted-suicide campaigners' aspirations are highly relevant to my own at the end of my mother's life. Time and again, we come across stories, some of which are related in this book, of people who find themselves convinced that they want to take their own lives, only to discover later that they are relieved beyond measure that they were prevented from doing so. And, regrettably, time and again we come across instances of laws being introduced in other countries on compassionate grounds, where the practice subsequently turns into death-on-request or euthanasia without consent, or worse – all of which is also recorded in this book.

I believe that development to be profoundly wrong. Yet when I write in opposition to assisted suicide, an alarming number of people write to me to say that they hope I die of an agonizing disease to serve me right, or that I'll develop a terminal disease that'll change my mind. That may give a truer indication of some of the alleged compassion in the pro-suicide lobby, but it is also at the root of what drives it. Fear leads us to consider that life can be treated as a consumer product, to be disposed of when it turns rotten, and to kid ourselves that there is "dignity" in doing so, rather than pouring our energy, resources and investment into our world-leading palliative care, a source of real dignity, all of which will be threatened if death becomes a clinical treatment option. To commoditize life is to disown it and to deny others their duty of care.

None of this is to deny the enormity and difficulty of death in our lives. For believer and non-believer alike, death is the biggest issue facing us and one, depending on your viewpoint, that influences much or all that precedes it. It's not good enough to oppose assisted suicide and euthanasia without arguing for something better. Nor is it good enough simply to argue for better palliative care as an alternative. Even enthusiasts for euthanasia support good palliative care (though I believe that experience shows us that this aspiration is eroded by euthanasia). What we need to do is to understand where our desire to legitimize assisted suicide comes from at the start of the twenty-first century and whether it can be justified. I believe that it cannot be so justified socially, culturally, politically, medically or religiously, and this book addresses all those factors.

But what of human suffering at the end of life? How do we make sense of that if we are to reject assisted suicide and euthanasia? This is not a book solely about theodicy, the theological practice that seeks to make sense of suffering in the context of an all-loving God, but of course it is informed by my Christian faith, as people are informed by other faiths or lack of any. There are atheists who are against assisted suicide, just as there are Christians who support it. Diversity in how we interpret our faith is one of the greatest pleasures and one of the most onerous burdens of being an Anglican. The privileges of our reformist tradition are often lost to us in the rows and alienations that can arise from this diversity, over issues such as human sexuality, which can threaten schism and exodus in favour of other, more prescriptive denominations.

So it is with assisted suicide. I must acknowledge openly, warmly and, indeed, in good faith, that there are Christians who support assisted suicide and even euthanasia. I can suggest, and will in this book, that I feel there are strong reasons for arguing that the antithetical position to my own is not a gospel that is recognizable, but just as soon as we start to suggest that any of us has proprietorship over that gospel is the moment that we start to lose it. I disagree, sometimes vehemently, with my fellow Christians but, with one or two extreme exceptions, I will not proscribe any view that diverges from my own as being beyond the reach and redemption of the God who owns all. To do so would be to deny the limitless value of being on a common journey of exploration of the gospel in the world we've been given and the notion that Christianity, in all its variety, is worth miraculously more than the sum of its parts.

One such Christian from whom I am in polarized disagreement over the issues of assisted suicide and euthanasia is Paul Badham. Like me, he is an Anglican priest. Unlike me, he is a distinguished theologian, as Professor of Theology and Religious Studies at the University of Wales, Lampeter. And, like me, he has written a book on a Christian approach to assisted suicide (entitled *Is There a Christian Case for Assisted Dying? Voluntary euthanasia reassessed*), the publication of which partly inspired me to write the repudiation that this book represents. So, unlike me, he concludes that there is a Christian case for assisted suicide. Again, like me, his opinions are forged by the experience of the last times and death of a dearly loved parent. Again, unlike me, that experience has substantially formed for him a case for supporting assisted suicide and euthanasia.

Professor Badham's father, Leslie Badham, was also a priest, a Royal Chaplain at Windsor, whose protracted and terrible terminal illness (he suffered prostate cancer for a decade until his death in 1975) has profoundly forged his son's support for an interpretive theology which, *inter alia*, argues the case for a loving and compassionate God who longs not only for us to be with him, but also that we should not unnecessarily suffer. Professor Badham acknowledges that his father was steeped in a different and sterner ecclesiology, from which his son wishes he could have been released.

It would be impertinent to intrude into the Badham family's suffering and grief any further. Suffice to say that Leslie Badham developed an inspirational (for me) theodicy, from which his son, witnessing his suffering, feels that he must demur. I will explore the theology of suffering in Chapter Five. However, it's not just about theology, of course. There are politics to be negotiated here, in the sense that not a few in the euthanasia debate will state that this is exactly the circumstance in which a degree of libertarian choice should be available. I may well see validity and inspiration in the bravely borne suffering of the Reverend Badham and may aspire to emulate it. But how dare I seek to inflict my choice on others who do not share my views and who may want to choose a quieter and more peaceful timing of their exit from this life?

The answer is that I don't seek to impose my view on others. I only ask that its validity or otherwise is considered alongside the views of Mr Badham and those who support assisted suicide and euthanasia. That is the purpose of this book. I happen to believe that assisted suicide and euthanasia are dangerous both in principle and practice, and of course I would hope that this view prevails in the democratic process. But I will respect decisions that go against my beliefs, so long as those decisions are taken properly in the legislative and democratic process. As matters stand and as we shall see in the course of this book, the practice of assisted suicide and euthanasia is sinisterly and perhaps cynically circumventing the democratic process and the will of the British Parliament. That is almost as worrying for me as the introduction of euthanasia itself to the UK, not least because it means that we may well be adopting practices that have proved at best shabby and at worst immoral in the United States and in continental Europe, practices that are also explored in detail in this book.

Furthermore, it would be more than impertinent of me, probably it would be inhuman, to suggest that anyone should suffer as the Reverend Badham did, in a manner of which I have no experience. As I have indicated, there are plenty of people who have publicly expressed the view that I will change my view just as soon as I'm screaming out in the pain of a terminal condition (charmingly, there are those too who publicly wish on me cancers and immobilizing disease simply because I hold the views that I do). In actuality, hospital evidence rather suggests that the process works the other way around; it is the healthy young and middle-aged who are enthusiastic about assisted suicide, while those who are old or are suffering from terminal diseases tend to recant their earlier support for an assisted death. The central thrust and thread of my argument in this book is that we should concentrate all our human effort on the relief of suffering, an effort that is undermined once death has become a clinical option.

In terms of direct experience of appalling suffering, it is true that my parents' deaths were not the same as the Reverend Badham's. Compared with his death, my parents had relatively "good" deaths. But, in the absence of the Reverend Badham being able to tell us whether it was all worth it, experience is all I have to go on. I am in no doubt that the playing out of life to its natural end is not just a worthwhile but a sacramental enterprise. Where Professor Badham is right is that the suffering that can be entailed in that process can neither be God's will for the faithful, nor acceptable and compassionate for the faithless. However, to my mind Professor Badham's experience provides an overpowering case for the extension of palliative care, literally to make dying easier, and against a consumerist provision of death as a clinical "treatment".

In saying that, I acknowledge that this is an immense social and political challenge. The National Council for Palliative Care estimates that the number of people dying annually in England and Wales is predicted to rise by 17 per cent over the next 20 years from about 503,000 (2006's figure) to about 586,000 in 2030. That equates to about 100,000 more people dying each year in the UK by 2030. That clearly has implications for public spending on palliative care and I take no whimsical view that budgets will be magically conjured. What I do know is that no politician should be encouraged in the idea that a solution to the care of our increasingly expensive elderly is to kill them.

Lastly, I must say something about my own priesthood. It all too often serves the purpose of those who would introduce euthanasia to the UK to characterize the debate as being between compassionate, secular rationalists and loony religious fundamentalists. That's not fair for a variety of reasons (not least among them that there are perfectly balanced people of faith, such as Professor Badham, who for rational reasons of their own support assisted suicide and euthanasia). Of course being a priest in the Anglican tradition – and never mind being a priest, simply being a Christian – is a major component in forming who I am. It informs my worldview and influences my decisions. But it doesn't dictate a set of rules or even rubrics for what I do or what I am. The Christian faith is a way of living which is constantly informed itself by the world in which we live. I see the world through the prism of my faith, but I also understand my faith through what goes on around me – as St Paul would say, "through a glass darkly". That's why this is not just a religious book. It looks at the cases against assisted suicide and euthanasia from the viewpoints of the legislature and the medical profession and from social and cultural perspectives. Faith is nothing on its own; it only begins to make sense in its relation to the world, in our relationships and in how we run the world. How we die is one aspect of how we live. This book is about how we might go about it, and I hope it leads to some conclusion as to how we should.

CHAPTER 1

IDOLS AND ICONS

Charlotte Raven, the author and polemicist, has tested positive for the incurable degenerative disease Huntington's. She writes of the sense of relief and liberation she feels when she realizes that she can kill herself. She describes her husband's opposition to her plans as "instinctual rather than intellectual. He couldn't offer any supporting evidence for his sense that a suffering, angry and dependent wife was better than a dead one." Then she visits a community of Huntington's sufferers in Venezuela and encounters the horrors of the disease in the context of families and those who care for them. A hug from one of the carers, Margarita Parra, proves a turning point: "In her arms, I feel like a rabbit being hugged by a teddy bear. I forget all my questions, which feels like a blessing... Registering the discomfort of existence, I felt a great wave of self-pity, the first since my diagnosis. I felt worthy of being cherished and knew I'd do whatever it took to survive. Back home, I told my husband he was right. The case for carrying on can't be argued. Suicide is rhetoric. Life is life."[1]

*

Raven is living, breathing proof that our lives only make sense and are only defined in our relationships with other people, whether they are close to us or not. Yet the most frequent response to an opposition to assisted suicide is a personalized and libertarian one. Like the response of Raven's husband to her proposed suicide, though very different in its conclusion, it is a visceral and intuitive reaction, confident in its assumption and outraged by any perceived challenge to its essential truth. It runs something like this: "How dare you tell me when and how I should die. My life is mine and mine alone, to live and end as I please. Nobody, least of all a busybody priest, will dictate to me that I should be kept alive."

There is a firm validity in the expression of this view. No human being, least of all that busybody priest, enjoys a hegemony over another. For the religious person, the created human is accountable only to his or her god, especially in the post-Reformation Christian doctrine of "justification by faith alone"; for the secular person, freedom to self-determination is the essential (ironically, almost the sacred), non-negotiable quality of human existence. A mixture of these two incontrovertible truths comprises a heady cocktail.

The weakness of this indignant challenge lies in what it fails to say and in the fragility of its provenance. It fails to acknowledge that there is a moral gulf between what we can do and what we have a right to do. We can own a house, or a car or a yacht, but we don't have a right to do so; similarly, we can take ownership of our own lives, but we don't have a right to do so, in the sense that we have a right to be free but we don't own freedom. To do so would create a thorny paradox: Freedom is an objective absolute for all; to take possession of it is to destroy it for others. There has to be some management of personal freedom, some mores that regulate it beyond the idea that you can do what you like so long as it doesn't damage others. As the Austrian statesman Prince Metternich put it: "Freedom cannot exist without the concept of order." Again, for the religious person, freedom is a gift of God and true freedom can only be found in faith. As St John records Jesus telling the Jews: "You will know the truth, and the truth will make you free" (John 8:32). For the secular person, freedom is enshrined in the state, at least in its democratic form, and cannot be annexed by the individual short of anarchy. This deconstruction of an intuitive assumption of freedom of choice and action leads us to decisions about what kind of world we want to live in, which is the subject of the next chapter.

First, we need to examine where this assumption of personal autonomy comes from. Such autonomy is only a fairly recent development in human history; a pre-Enlightenment, Western worldview would assume that individuals have a pre-eminent corporate responsibility – an assumption which, however, had some fairly revolting manifestations in religious and political control structures. Eastern, particularly Japanese, ethics of autonomy would admittedly take a different view; with regard to suicide, the Samurai tradition would impute the notion of honour, regulated by obedience to superiors. But the oppressions of the medieval and ancient past in the West do not prescribe that post-Enlightenment models are 'more virtuous. We may have moved on but we may not have cracked a paradigm of human liberty – indeed, the evidence of the contemporary world, from Guantanamo Bay to pettifogging attempts in the UK to introduce identity cards and a national DNA database, would suggest otherwise. The intuitive assumption of personal self-determination, with its inalienable right to ownership of one's own life, to live and dispose of as we please, owes its existence less to any crafted political philosophy than to an abstract co-incidence of post-Enlightenment anti-religiosity, post-modern individualism and human-rights legislation that has spawned a libertarian industry, the ambient noise of which has decreed that our bodies only belong to their tenants, a truth which we take to be self-evident, but which is profoundly wrong.

The individual is born

It's too crass a generalization to suggest that the eighteenth-century Enlightenment was responsible for the emergence of a cult of the individual. Socrates and the classical Greek philosophers knew the power of the individual for self-determination (and Socrates was, of course, a famous suicide). But there's little doubt that for Enlightenment philosophers individualism was an idea whose time had come. Combined with the work of John Stuart Mill on free will and Immanuel Kant on rationalism, the idea that the human being could and should have management control of his own destiny was a premise on which subsequent Western economics and politics have been constructed.

Individualist thinkers of the Enlightenment didn't necessarily believe that individuals should have entirely unfettered autonomy over their own lives. Jean-Jacques Rousseau argued that the state has a role in the furtherance of the individual's interests; in his model, the law enhances the benefits of the individual, as to live an unlawful life would be to indulge irrational passions at the cost of the individual's autonomy of reason, which is the higher form of human existence. But individualism nevertheless largely takes it for granted that the individual knows best what is good for him and that the state, society or other forms of authority should butt out. It's a line of thinking that has its contemporary equivalent in the blogging libertarian, particularly the polemical, neo-con blogger of the United States, who claims that his life is his own possession, to do with as he pleases and, so long as no one else is adversely affected, he should be left to his own devices.

Utilitarianism, as a philosophical school under the tutelage of Jeremy Bentham and J. S. Mill, also played its role in the establishment of personal autonomy. Usually utilitarianism is described in shorthand as the moral worth of an action quantified as "being of the greatest good to the greatest number of people". Negative utilitarianism speaks of morality measured by the least evil being caused by a negative action, or by preventing the greatest amount of suffering for the most people through a course of moral action. One can quite easily see how these lines of thought can be co-opted, as a deliberate action or simply as part of a prevailing *zeitgeist*, to support the idea that the removal of oneself from the world is a moral action if it serves the interests of most people connected with, say, the terminally ill (family, medical staff, or the majority of the British public that is said to support assisted suicide). Or, to take the negative utilitarian line, it would surely be an act of high moral worth to avoid the "evil" of suffering unbearable pain, as well as to save the suffering of those family members who have to witness it, if the terminally ill were to take a Socratic draught.

On these kinds of Enlightenment platforms stand, some four

centuries later, the justifications for the moral worth of assisted suicide and euthanasia, for which it is axiomatic not only that the individual is the first and only judge of when the time is right for dying, but that there is a greater good being served for society and for those on whom the dying are a painful and distressing burden (whether that is true or not, it will form a part of the moral action of the terminally ill in ending their lives) by choosing the moment of their premature departure.

But if the Enlightenment was a kind of unlocking of the armoury of individualism, it wasn't until the second half of the twentieth century that the weapons were turned on the collectivists and the idea that a human life could be the property or responsibility of anyone else other than the person who lives it.

The wars of the twentieth century exhibited levels of self-sacrifice for others, for nationhood, freedom and ideology which spawned a reactive concentration on individualistic liberty; freedom for *us* at the start of the century had become freedom for *me* by its close. It's one reason why Tony Blair found it harder to take our country to war in Iraq than Winston Churchill did against Germany, the latter being unlikely to face a million-strong, anti-war demonstration, even if that number of pacifists and appeasers existed in 1939. The two world wars, especially the Great War, had also swept aside the social structures that had, in one form or another, endured since feudal times. At worst, these had been exploitative and oppressive; at best, they had entrenched societal principles of duty to others, responsibility and service and a common bond of nationhood under God. Lives were not an individualistic possession; they were lived in the service of family, society, nation and God. Lives could also be brutal and short by modern standards, but church and state co-extended sufficiently to enjoy both a benign and an abusive control over individual human lives.

By the halfway mark of the twentieth century, this quasi-eucharistic way of living one's life, as a sacrifice for others and for the common good, was disintegrating. A thousand-year model of king-and-country, first in the notion of "England" and later reaching its apotheosis in the British Empire during the nineteenth century, was found inadequate and increasingly pointless. The British Empire was in retreat, the locus of imperial power moving to the United States, with its written constitution that elevated the freedom of the individual to at least a similar status to the interests of the nation state and the service of it. The individual's right to life, liberty and the pursuit of happiness was the new world rubric, emanating from the developed Judaeo-Christian West, and usurping the old rallying cry of "For England, Harry and St George".

Growing economic prosperity after the Second World War began to provide the kind of individual freedom that enabled people to break away from the expectations of nation and society. The rise of the individual found a momentum in the counter-cultural, social-revolutionary movement known as "the Sixties". At a distance of half a century, the Sixties are widely perceived as being less about a self-generating miracle of fresh and youthful energy directed at replacing a bunch of war-mongering squares and fogies, and more about the triumph of a selfish individualism at the cost of self-awareness.

Popular music attacked materialism and the establishment, while founding a new aristocracy of celebrity that, by the millennium, had produced a society in which rock stars join the political set to manage the world economy, the prevalent ambition of school-leavers is to achieve fame and celebrity, irrespective of what they actually do for a living, and young people try to impress others by claiming that they are in a band, as they once did by saying they were in the armed forces. The Sixties and the baby-boom they supported were the maternity wards for this new culture, a place where anti-materialist demi-gods such as the Beatles could concurrently be the highest-paid entertainers on the planet and sing "All You Need Is Love". For all its pretence that working-class heroes were leading a way to a new co-operative Nirvana, this was principally a middle-class affair. Workers could ill afford the new self-indulgences of the Sixties, while flower-power boys and girls from mock-Tudor homes in Surrey smoked pot and shopped at Biba.

The drugs were said to raise consciousness, but in reality (albeit an altered one) led their regular users to inhabit their own little world of self-entertainment, the organic and narcotic equivalent of an iPod. The anti-war movement was about bloody confrontations over a war in south-east Asia that few demonstrators knew anything about. Led by those who could afford not to work or to maintain themselves at college, it was a revolt against "the pigs" – police officers who, unlike the protesters, had to earn a living. Feminism, whose founding sisterhood had liberated women from the oppression of the stove and the shorthand notebook, gave birth to the bastard child that is the commoditization of sex, the freedom to look and to be available, the strident individualism that gave us the high-capitalistic Spice Girls, rightful heiresses to the commercial pop con-trick of the Sixties, and hedonistic ladettes flaunting their girl-power with their heads emetically between their knees in bus-lanes of provincial towns on a Saturday night. This was not Generation X, it was Natasha Walter's Living Dolls and it was the Me Generation – actually two generations: the right-on freedom-fighters of the Sixties producing babies that knew no better by way of parental role models than to accrue as much of what makes you feel good as you can, because if it feels good you should do it.

It was into the still-youthful lives of the Sixties generation that Margaret Thatcher marched. Mocked by the sophisticated rock 'n' rollers and all who fancied that they led an "alternative" lifestyle, such as the comedians telling daring gags about body-parts and dreaming of a series with the BBC, Mrs Thatcher nevertheless gave them what they wanted. She issued their licence to print money. They didn't need to know about Milton Friedman's pre-eminence over Keynesian economics, nor did they need to know that they were being sold state assets that they already owned, in order to have their taxes cut, nor that home-ownership was to become a form of graven-image idolatry that would lead the financial institutions that supported it to very nearly collapsing the world economy within a generation. They simply needed to know that they could have all they wanted if they used their own initiative.

It was only natural that this quest for instant gratification should translate from the materialistic to the spiritual and metaphysical; in this worldview, religion is judged on what is in it for me, rather than for those I love. It's a short skip and a jump to the variety of New Age spiritualities that emerged from more ancient practices during the last two decades of the twentieth century. The crystal-clutching and druidic tree-hugging was really just another manifestation of the new faith in consumerism that emerged in the boom years of the Eighties, which bore the designer label "conspicuous consumption". If I have a wealth of consumer choice in the things I desire to enrich my material person, why would the same not apply to my spiritual self, that element of my human identity that isn't visible in my choice of clothes and motor-cars? Post-modern pick 'n' mix religion was born, the constituent parts of which were to combine to make me the kind of person I wish to be, rather than the unique human being I am wished to be. And, naturally (for the proponent of this argument), it's a short walk in the superstore of consumerism from the spiritual gondolas, with real gods stacked temptingly by the more idolatrous products of a have-it-all society, to the cosy café in which it is a truth universally acknowledged that I can choose the manner and timing of my death, just as I choose where and when I go on holiday.

It may not be very tempting for many of us to give Baroness Thatcher the benefit of the doubt, but where we've arrived may well not have been the destination she intended when she set us on the journey with free markets, deregulation, privatization and all the other apparatus of the neo-liberal economic policies that indelibly stamped her regime on British post-war history. She did say to *Woman's Own* magazine in 1987 that "there is no such thing as society", but the context of that remark is everything, as it invariably is. What she said was this:

> I think we've been through a period where too many
> people have been given to understand that if they have a
> problem, it's the government's job to cope with it. "I have
> a problem, I'll get a grant." "I'm homeless, the government
> must house me." They're casting their problem on society.
> And, you know, there is no such thing as society. There

are individual men and women, and there are families.
And no government can do anything except through
people, and people must look to themselves first. It's our
duty to look after ourselves and then, also to look after
our neighbour. People have got the entitlements too
much in mind, without the obligations. There's no such
thing as entitlement, unless someone has first met an
obligation.

She was not saying that she, or an accident of history, had atomized society. She most definitely was not denying societal obligation; if anything, her small-town Methodism shines through the phrase "look after our neighbour", even if she does subordinate it to looking after ourselves (which may lead us rationally to an inversion of the Christian golden rule: Love yourself as you love your neighbour). A full reading of this pithy insight into Thatcherite philosophy reveals that she is a child of Enlightenment individualism, the heiress of Rousseau, able to assimilate her passions for the Conservative commitment to law and order only through the cold reason that the individual's quality of life and prospects are enhanced by doing so. The individual still rules supreme in her universe. If Thatcher is to be quoted in this context, it's as an individualist in the Enlightenment tradition.

The problem for Thatcherism was that those individual men and women privatized themselves. They bought back their stock from the state, floated themselves and their homes on the Stock Market through their securitized and ultimately sub-prime and toxic mortgages and withdrew their assets from society. They got the individualistic bit, but dispensed with the Thatcherite neighbourly part. Into the Nineties, well after Mrs Thatcher had left to spend more time with her ideology, Gordon Gekko's greed-is-good cult started to mainline on its hedge-funded lifestyle. The Me Generation became the Gimme Generation. There was no turning back after the lady who was "not for turning".

Maybe it was society that became poisoned. Maybe it was just a bunch of individuals who were poisoned, or who administered their own lethal injection. But by the millennium something was dying – and not with dignity. What for thousands of years had been revered as the sanctity of life had developed a death rattle. A ghostly pallor was on the cheeks of the age-old idea that every life was of equal and limitless value. If everything else in the span of our human existence was tradable and biddable, if all life's products and services, from healthcare and water-supply to education and prison services, even spirituality and other "quality time" activities, then why could death not be bought and sold? Truly free markets started to offer us not just the life we wanted, but the death as well, delivered as one of our entrepreneurial service industries. Life and death had been commoditized.

Human rights and wrongs

These years of plenty in the second half of the twentieth century, after the storms of the first half, presented us with one ancillary challenge: Where to park up the liberal conscience. Many aspects of liberalism were highly desirable in the new Western world order. Economic liberalism was deemed by the new individualists to be very good indeed. Even a lot of social liberalism served the purposes of neo-liberalism; think of the "pink pound" and the attractions to both partners of a marriage being brought into the earning power of the workplace, with the female of the pair back at work as quickly as possible after childbirth. Apart from anything else, we could double the size of our mortgages. That was one aspect of social liberalism that was as cunning as it was attractive; dressed up as a "freedom of choice", it actually removed the choice not to work for women with children who had joint mortgages to service, and fuelled the very house-price inflation that they had borrowed to take advantage of in the first place. Liberalism served the free markets in ways beyond the principles only of economic liberalism.

But where in this economy do you put the liberal conscience, with all its irritating concerns for the vulnerable, the infirm, the oppressed and the marginalized? Well, it turned out that you could incorporate it. Step forward the human-rights industry.

Human rights, like freedom, are undoubtedly A Good Thing. One could no more be against human rights than for child labour. On balance, it's hard to summon up any substantial censure for 1948's Universal Declaration of Human Rights from the United Nations, with its "recognition [that] the inherent dignity and of the equal and inalienable rights of all members of the human family is the foundation of freedom, justice and peace in the world."

But, again like a virtuous abstract such as freedom, an unbridled reinterpretation by selfish interests can lead to unintended consequences. A minor and irritating example of such consequences is the tribe of lawyers coaxing their clientele to the European Court of Human Rights, for motives not entirely to do with their appellants' best interests. A more serious consequence than the avarice of briefs, however, is the prevalence in common consciousness of rights and privileges over responsibilities, which further fuelled a growing obsession with personal autonomy.

This observation is all too often abrogated by the political Right. It is a favourite chant of Righties to repeat the words "human rights" as though the phrase is a pejorative, whenever qualities of soft individualism or social justice are called for, rather than the hard, self-determinist variety of which they approve. Similar phrases, such as "political correctness" and "elf 'n' safety" (note the hilarious play on the common tongue there), are wheeled out whenever unbridled liberty is threatened with constraint.

The business of human rights warrants a place here because of the societal psychology that it generates. It is widely held as a universal truth, and not just among libertarians, that we have a right to anything that does no one else any harm. This is close to, if not indistinguishable from, the "right" to have anything I want, so long as there is no deleterious effect on others. This is patently absurd. I have no right to a castle in Scotland. We have no right to a life free of debilitating disease. We have no right to have children, though the lengths of IVF treatment and, worse, the expression of gender-preference for offspring and tearful performances from the childless in the media, are evidence that some couples (and even some singles) are persuaded otherwise.

If there are some conditions of life that we consider happenstance, providence, good or bad fortune, a gift, or simply chemical serendipity, then there is a simple extension of this rationale: We have no human right to the death of our choice. We may desire one, we may even manage our life in such a way as to engineer one, but the idea that taking our own life is a right is one that has erroneously emerged in the post-modern climate since suicide was decriminalized in 1961. What society does not condemn, it does not necessarily approve. There is any number of human actions, particularly in the arena of human sexuality and its commercialization, that we might condemn, or censure, or of which we disapprove, but, in a free and democratic society, that we do not outlaw. Take prostitution. Or indeed suicide. Our society offers legal sanction against neither. But that does not bestow on us a human right, simply a lawful one, to hire lap-dancers or watch pornography. Or to take our own lives. At its simplest, a legal right is not necessarily a moral, or consequently a human, right.

There are those who would claim that human rights are justified by their essential negativity. They are "freedoms from" harm rather than "passports to" desires. I'm not sure about that. I believe we do have desires that should be enshrined in human rights – a passport to life, liberty and the pursuit of happiness just about covers it.

But of greater concern to me is the assumption that simply what I want can and should be pursued in human rights legislation. It's a dangerous mindset that imbues our legislature. In 2009, multiple-sclerosis sufferer Debbie Purdy successfully took her appeal to the (now abolished) Law Lords, to demand legislative guidance as to whether her partner would be prosecuted under the Suicide Act 1961 if he assisted her to kill herself when she decided she could bear her condition no longer.

I am regularly (and I suspect sometimes deliberately) misunderstood on this specific issue. Let me be clear: I take absolutely no issue with Ms Purdy pursuing this case. It is entirely right that a citizen should be enabled to challenge the legislature, in a parliamentary democracy. That is even her human right, if you like, though I might take issue with the answer she received.

It is the vocabulary of human rights in the Law Lords' ruling that is unsettling. They said she had the right to choose how she died, under Article 8 of the European Convention on Human Rights:

> Everyone has the right to respect for their private life and the way that Ms Purdy determines to spend the closing moments of her life is part of the act of living. Ms Purdy wishes to avoid an undignified and distressing end to her life. She is entitled to ask that this too must be respected.[2]

So European human rights legislation, as articulated by the Law Lords, trumps the British law on suicide, which holds that no one can aid or abet a fellow human being to kill themselves. Simply what someone wants for themselves must be protected as sacrosanct. Individual desire has triumphed over act of Parliament. I'm fairly sure that this is not where the human rights movement intended to take us.

The body's image

It is all too tempting for the faithful to become misty-eyed with nostalgia for the pre-Enlightenment centuries, the Renaissance beauty of a transcendent God and a medieval era that innocently and intuitively understood the Augustinian synthesis between faith and reason, where no one of education would consider that rationalism was an antithesis to religious faith. It's tempting, but wrong. We should not theologically romanticize the past. There was nothing enviable, nor sacramental, about birth as a percentage game of survival against the odds of heinous levels of child mortality, the mortal risks for women inherent in that childbirth, the casual oppressions of the physically powerful, the lack of hygiene and health, the bubonic boils and lack of medicine, and a life expectancy of two or three decades if you were lucky enough to pull through most of those dangers.

The quality of life – and its quantity – have been immeasurably enriched, at least in the developed world, in the modern era. Modern medicine and palliative care, access to enhanced diets and clean water, the isolation of infection, antibiotics and proprietary drugs, the relative absence of war, the rule of democratic law to protect us all from violence, and a degree of control over natural disaster; these have all pushed our Western, average life expectancy out from thirty or forty years as recently as the early twentieth century, to the early seventies now. These figures can be misleading; if you survived your teenage years before the twentieth century, your life expectancy was not far off what we enjoy today. And there were colossal variations according to class, occupation and the incidence of disease. But what we do know is that many more of us, in the developed West, are living longer.

The baby-boom, post-war generation and improved medical care have delivered us an elderly bulge in the population that isn't going to go away. Indeed, this is a plank in the platform on which pro-assisted suicide enthusiasts stand. Not, you understand, that their case for helping the old to die should cynically be characterized as a culling of the inconvenient and expensive members of our society in their twilight years, because they are a drag on the resources of the able-bodied. No, it's more a question of setting out an altogether more (apparently) compassionate proposition that the elderly with terminal conditions should not artificially be kept alive by the wonders of modern science, when they want and are going to die anyway, and that science should be turned to their assistance and the fulfilment of their wishes for extinction, rather than to the prolongation of their suffering. The antithesis to that is complex and is further explored in Chapter Four.

For now, I want to concentrate simply on the idea that we should not necessarily want to bin everything about the pre-Enlightenment mindset, or that we shouldn't be too keen to throw the medieval baby out with the post-modern bathwater. We should not, perhaps, use these historical labels too liberally; "medieval" is very often used as a pejorative. Non-believers will often claim that my faith is "medieval nonsense", as if its very antiquity invalidates it (it's not even as if, in human terms, it's that old – and in evolutionary terms Jesus Christ was born a couple of minutes ago). Drop the labels of historical periods and we see more clearly that humanity has been thinking about living and dying and what it means to be here and human for a very long time. That's a reservoir of thought that we fail to tap at our peril.

But this book is not a module in a Masters degree in medieval theology (thank God). It is just an excursion into what Christianity has had to say about the quality of human life and what it is for. In this section, I want to say something about the image of God in humanity, life as a gift and living as service.

Imago Dei is the theological thread through human history that holds, *inter alia*, that we humans are created in God's image. In short (which is always difficult in these circumstances), bearing the image of God means that we each have a unique value and purpose in our lives that transcend our utility and function as biological human beings. This is, of course, the natural language of the religious, but it has to be said at the outset that people of faith don't have and should not claim to have a monopoly over this doctrine. Secular humanists, human rights campaigners and even, or especially, the don't-knows will and do concur with the one-sentence definition I offer above, probably with the God bit taken out: Every human life is of unique and limitless value and should be cherished, treasured and defended, even (again, especially) when that life is frail or vulnerable, oppressed or *in extremis*, or the object of contempt and marginalization. I have many friends, for example, who feel no divine vocation in their tireless work of befriending and defending people who have committed the most terrible murders and await execution on the world's Death Rows. This altruistic motivation, this idea that there is something divine about the human condition, is very often abbreviated as "the sanctity of life", but it is far from being the property of the household of faith. Indeed, the faithful weaken their faith if they claim anything other than that every human is made in the image of God, regardless of their creed or circumstance. Nobody is a bit more or less in that image – it is an absolute or it is nothing. We could use "sanctity of life", but that is essentially to introduce weasel-words where the traditional term is *Imago Dei*, so with a degree of robust candour it is with the image of God that I proceed here.

As we are made in the image of God, it would seem to follow that we enjoy a special, divine investment in humanity and its journey through time, an investment that is not to be found elsewhere in creation. The dividend on this investment is a consciousness of our spirituality, our mission and our mortality, a consciousness that is not apparently to be found elsewhere in creation, as the ancient, mythological creation narrative of Genesis endeavours to adumbrate. This is an important distinction of the human from other animals; the stewardship of the Earth with which we are entrusted includes a responsibility for the mortality of animals, an issue I will return to in Chapter Four.

The relationship between a creator God and his created humanity is bound to be an infinitely complex and mysterious one, in that it matches a divine perfection with a humanity that is clearly very far from perfect, God's infallibility with our fallibility, often called a "fallen" state. For Christians, this relationship finds its most intimately carnal fulfilment in the life, death and resurrection of Jesus Christ, in whom God and humanity meet at the Cross, an incarnation that we struggle to understand as both fully God and fully human, as humanity has struggled to understand its divinity since the Patriarchs. With them, we endeavour to establish that true and complete humanness contains a true divinity, just as divinity now contains a humanness in Christ. Top-down, as it were, God has achieved this in a kenotic way – the *kenosis* being the Greek word for the way in which the Godhead empties himself of his divinity in the Christ. Bottom-up, meanwhile, we reflect the divine in our lives, in our abilities to be creative and to be conscious of our mortality, most importantly to love unconditionally in the manner in which we are loved and through the experience and appreciation of transcendence and immanence.

But Christians argue that we can't achieve any of this on our own.

We can be truly human and express divinity in our humanity only in our relationships with each other in our mortal lives, which at their most sacramental reflect our relationship with God. We can only be known, to others and fully to ourselves, in our interaction with other people. It is how we are known and defined. The process is supported by the infinitely complex way in which God reveals himself and is known to us; not only through the incarnation of and our relationship with the living Christ, but in the theological modelling, through the ages, of constructs to enable us to understand the nature and being of God. Take the relationship between the three persons of the Trinity as understood through history – the Father, the Son and the Holy Spirit, who are at once discrete and coterminous as one, at once independent and utterly co-dependent. A bit like us, really. So, paradoxically, we become more or even most human when we become most like the Christ, in a unity with one creator God and the enabling Holy Spirit, and least human when we lose touch with that Godhead.

The relevance of all this to the assisted suicide and euthanasia debates is twofold: Our lives are only fully understood and completed in the context of them having been gifted to us in the first place, and through our gifting of them to other people as we live them and, indeed, as we leave them.

So, wrapped in the concept that we are created in the image of God is the fairly obvious implication that our lives are gifted to us. It would be a strange, callous and ungrateful recipient of a present who threw such a precious gift away. Yet we might, of course, dispose of any gift from a loved one when it has become old and broken and decayed, however much we have appreciated having it and having been given it. Surely the giver would understand and, indeed, approve. I address the nature of the value of life at its end in Chapter Six. But at this stage we just need to acknowledge that the idea behind *Imago Dei* is that life has been gifted to us, as an act of unconditional and incarnational love, and that the gift is an incalculably precious one.

Furthermore, our lives, if they are to have any meaning, are gifted by us to others in acts of love that reflect at the mortal level the divine act of creation. Again, the life of Christ offers the model for fulfilment: "For the Son of Man came not to be served but to serve" (Mark 10:45). Our human identity is wrapped up in, indeed entirely dependent upon, our relationships with other people and, in particular, those we love and serve and those who love and serve us. The antithesis of this view – the one held by those who advocate the autonomous right to terminate one's own life at the time of our own choosing – is that we are autonomous individuals, defined by our own existence irrespective of our dependence on others and their dependence on us. That is a deeply depressing creed. As Vincent Nichols, Archbishop of Westminster, puts it: "This is surely the triumph of the philosophy that proclaims individual rights above all other considerations and the relativist insistence that what is good is a matter of personal judgment."[3]

I have traced some of the causes of the rise of this attitude: the development of individualism; the Sixties hippy-hegemony of "self"; the assumption of consumerist "choice" which prospered in a neo-liberal economy; a particular strain of human rights legislation that enshrines the freedom of the individual over responsibility to the other. They are consequences of the obsession with self and the desire for complete autonomy over one's destiny. Archbishop Nichols summarizes some of them as the weakening of social structures, including the decline of the family as the core unit, the rise of antisocial behaviour, the pursuit of profit at all costs and the increasing intolerance of non-materialist, philosophical or ethical views: "It can be summarised as the age of convenience; the pursuit of what we want despite its cost and impact on others."[4]

Convenience-shopping for our own deaths is just another symptom of a self-obsessed society that takes it for granted that we are masters of our own lifespans, self-medicating and self-ending them. There are alternative views: that human life is not just something we produce, whether through sexual intercourse or in a laboratory, as a commodity like any other. The evidence of human existence – the awe and wonder displayed by newborn babies, or the instinctive sense of a duty of care for the weak, the ill and the elderly – suggests otherwise.

It is those instincts of serving our fellow human beings that are at stake when we commoditize human life.

The danger is that we are reductive of the quality of human life, just at the point that we seek to protect that quality by ending it when we choose, when we decide that the product has deteriorated to the point that we no longer want it. At this product level, the value of life is seen only in terms of quality control. And the prospect of euthanasia becomes no more demanding of our conscience than a visit to the recycling bins. But we need to ask who is the arbitrator of the quality of life, who is to decide when the human product is no longer of sufficient value to preserve, or is of inferior value by some arbitrary measure of able-bodied friends, family and, indeed, strangers. The answer from most euthanasia enthusiasts is that the individual is to decide for themselves. But that is deeply unsatisfactory, for it has already created the premise that some lives are, by virtue of their proximity to death, of lower value than others. All the individual has to decide is when that stage is reached, rather than if there is ever such a stage. Where, in this equation, is the value that is placed on enduring love and selfless care for those in distress and pain? And the comfort and relief of that pain, beyond the solution of snuffing out the life of the one who bears it, as the highest imperative of love?

The question, ultimately, is one of objective value. Archbishop Nichols asks rhetorically: "If my life has no objective value, then why should anyone else care for it?"[5] His point is that the notion of an absolute right to choose "a good death" may sound libertarian but it undermines society's commitment to support fellow members in adversity. And it encourages the abandonment of the ailing.

What he calls "the horizon of hope" is dramatically reduced at the point that life becomes entirely subject to human decision in its beginnings and endings. This does, of course, have the profoundest implications for abortion policy – a point one would expect to be raised by a Roman Catholic primate – but that is not the subject of this book. The point with regard to decisions of end-of-life timing is that autonomy is a chimera. We may believe that we are in complete autonomous control. Far more likely, though, is that someone else close to us, or in a professional medical role, will be taking that decision on our behalf. In Archbishop Nichols' phrase: "Once the coin of sovereignty over death has been minted, then it will be claimed by not a few."[6]

There is no Thatcherite free market, no retail experience, no fundamental human right, no notion that there is a pure individualism that grants us dominion over the creation and the taking of life. The spiritual dimension of humanity isn't like that. Only by denying that dimension entirely is it possible to talk in terms of having a "right" to take one's own life at the time of one's own choosing.

Archbishop Nichols quotes the poet Lucretius in this context: "Life is given to no one as freehold; we all hold it on leasehold."[7] You don't have to be religious to hold that view. You just have to be a human being – one who has lived and loved in community, one whose existence has changed the world forever by touching others' lives. That's why our deaths don't belong to us any more than our lives do. I offer the last word here to Archbishop Nichols:

> Dying is the most important step a person takes, for it
> is a step towards the ultimate fulfillment of our innate
> spiritual nature, our capacity to know God, to know the
> fullness of the mystery of all things. We have been created
> with this capacity and our best guide for living is to do
> nothing to dent, pervert or deaden it... Accepting that life
> is a gift is a good start. Sadly these centuries-old truths
> about the nature of humanity are no longer common
> currency. But we can surely all of us recognise, whether
> we approach our lives with or without a transcendental
> faith, the serious ethical and social dangers to which the
> doctrine of unfettered personal autonomy is leading us.[8]

And, indeed, that destination should be as worrying for those who have no faith as for those who do.

Notes

1. *The Guardian*, 16 January 2010.
2. Law Lords' ruling, July 2009.
3. *Daily Telegraph*, 16 July 2009.
4. Ibid.
5. Ibid.
6. Ibid.
7. Ibid.
8. Ibid.

CHAPTER 2

THE KILLING FIELDS

Just before Christmas 2009 a civil servant, whose working life has been spent at the heart of government, sent me a message at the *Daily Telegraph*, along with some helpful information:

> As you will know, the Dutch drift to legalised euthanasia began, in 1984, with guidelines for non-prosecution. The main difference between their experience and what is happening now in Britain is that Dutch doctors were persuaded to be compliant from the start: it was the KNMG, the Dutch equivalent of the BMA, that produced the criteria for acceptable euthanasias. The British medical establishment, by contrast, has shown itself to be made of sterner stuff – as a recent article by you eloquently pointed out – and [Director of Public Prosecutions] Keir Starmer's guidelines are not clinical guidelines.

This is gentle Whitehall-speak for "We don't want to make the mistakes that they have abroad." This chapter is dedicated to that civil servant – you know who you are.

*

In the previous chapter we examined some of the philosophical and socio-economic influences that have delivered us an environment in which assisted suicide and euthanasia might be considered acceptable, or even desirable. These might be described as upstream factors, as they are the source of a mindset in which the taking of human life becomes justifiable.

It's now time to consider the practice of assisted suicide and euthanasia downstream, as it were, at the point of delivery. We should ask ourselves: Do the proponents of assisted suicide consider that what actually happens in jurisdictions that tolerate some form of voluntary euthanasia is what they hoped for, or serves as a model for the responsible introduction of the practice elsewhere?

The initial indications are not good. It is estimated, for instance, that as many as one in four assisted suicides in Oregon are performed on patients who are clinically depressed.[1] I shall examine in some detail the implementation practice of assisted suicide in the three foreign jurisdictions that are best known for it and which are often held as examples of best practice: Oregon in the United States and, in Europe, the Netherlands and Switzerland.

State-endorsed assisted suicide is a relatively recent phenomenon in Western culture, partly for the post-modern and consumerist reasons already outlined, and partly through a growing secularization which has usurped a former, somewhat authoritarian Judaeo-Christian culture. As assisted suicide has crept into Western legislatures and gained a formal foothold, we should take stock and examine whether it is a progressive contribution to our society, or something more retrograde and sinister. I will come towards what the secularist might call utopian and what the Christian might call "Kingdom" values at the end of this chapter. But first we must examine the practical and political weaknesses of assisted suicide and euthanasia in those jurisdictions where they are legally permitted. Has the experience been beneficial? I will start in Oregon.

The Oregon experience

Oregon, where assisted suicide has been legal since 1998, is regularly held as a paragon of good practice, with no great increase in the incidence of suicide and solid protection for the vulnerable from coercion or manipulation. The Oregon Death with Dignity Act (ODDA, 1998) is an important influence on the UK legislature, because it formed the model for Lord Joffe's unsuccessful Assisted Dying for the Terminally Ill Bill of 2006, which was defeated in the House of Lords. Like the Oregon ODDA, the ADTI Bill allowed for assisted suicide, but not for voluntary euthanasia, though the declared intention of some campaigners is to reach voluntary euthanasia by legislative increments, of which an assisted-suicide Act would be the most significant. Building on the Oregon experience, the ADTI Bill proposed that doctors, at the request of a terminally ill adult, in the words of Dignity in Dying, "could prescribe life-ending medication, but they would not be able to administer it directly. Patients would have to take the medication themselves".[2] (Note the fascinating and slippery use of vocabulary here: "medication" is used in a context never previously known to the medical profession – this is a lethal dose of poison.)

Dignity in Dying, which campaigns for the introduction of assisted suicide into British law, declares confidently on its website (as of October 2009):

> When the law changes in Britain it is essential that there are sufficient legal safeguards to protect vulnerable people, as is the case in Oregon (USA). By providing safeguarded choice, the new law will ensure that vulnerable people are better protected than under the present status quo... Dignity in Dying believes that the debate on assisted dying is not about whether we should change the law, as this is beyond doubt, but rather what safeguards should be contained in a new Bill.[3]

Note that Dignity in Dying states that the case for a change in British law to accommodate assisted dying on the Oregon model "is beyond doubt", apparently. Beware any organization, including the religious, which claims that its ideology is beyond doubt. Dignity in Dying goes on to say that the Oregon ODDA "has worked successfully for 10 years", that there is no evidence of abuse "or the so-called 'slippery slope'" and that "the numbers using the [ODDA] to die are low and steady – and in 10 years just 341 people have been assisted to die, but many more have taken comfort from knowing the option is there". Those are big claims, particularly the almost miraculous ability of Dignity in Dying to know that an unspecified, though large, number of people have found comfort in simply knowing some legislation exists. These claims deserve investigation. I'm happy to oblige, because the Oregon experience is not all that it seems.

The Oregon Health Department (OHD) has (at the time of writing) issued eleven reports on the effect of the ODDA, one for each calendar year since its inception, 1998 to 2008 inclusive. Numbers taking their own lives under the Act have been on an upswing since 1998. Dignity in Dying is right to say that there were 341 reported suicides under the ODDA during the first decade of the legislation. What Dignity in Dying is careful not to say is that in the eleventh year, 2008, there were 60 suicides, by far the most since the ODDA was introduced and a sharp increase on the previous year's figure of 49. So the total that Dignity in Dying should be carrying on its website since the ODDA was introduced is not 341, but 401, an increase of well over 17 per cent in the latest year alone for which statistics are available. The rates of increase under the ODDA in Oregon are actually quite steep: From 24 to 88 lethal prescriptions since 1998 and from 16 to 60 suicides. (Obviously not all lethal doses are consumed in the year of their prescription.) Not quite the "low and steady" rates of suicide that Dignity in Dying would have us believe, and one wonders why this lobbying organization shrinks from presenting the figures in this rather more stark way.

(Stop Press: As this book went to publication, the OHD figures for 2009 were published, showing that the sharp spike in assisted suicides in 2008 is holding steady – there were 59 in 2009, against 60 the previous year. Meanwhile, Dignity in Dying continues to carry the 341 figure for the first 10 years, while the true figure is 460 deaths in 12 years, with very nearly a quarter of that total occurring in the past two years alone. In other words, what Dignity in Dying should be telling us is that the total for the first 10 years will be reached in half that time at the rate of the past two years. And that's if the rate holds at the current level. Again, this demolishes Dignity in Dying's claim for a "low and steady" rate of suicide in Oregon.)

Furthermore, the figures are presented as being statistically fairly insignificant (though, to be clear, no one in this debate is suggesting that even a single suicide is insignificant in human terms), without any proportional reference to population size. Oregon's population is just 3.8 million; the UK has some 61.5 million. If Oregon's experience is proportionally calculated for the UK, we would have had a rise over the period from 1998 to 2008 (while Dignity in Dying chooses to avoid the embarrassment of the spike in assisted suicides in 2008–9 – see above) of 389 to 1,426 lethal prescriptions issued, while assisted suicides would have risen from 259 to 972. The latter projected increase has eerie resonances of the 120 or so Britons who have killed themselves in the Dignitas clinic in Switzerland and the 800 who are said to be awaiting legal clearance.

More sinister is the admission from the OHD that it may not, in any event, be giving a clear picture of levels of assisted suicide in Oregon. The first 1998 report states:

> we cannot detect or collect data on issues of con-compliance with any accuracy. A 1995 anonymous survey of Oregon physicians found that 7% of surveyed physicians had provided prescriptions for lethal medication to patients prior to legalisation. We do not know if covert physician-assisted suicide continued to be practised in Oregon in 1998.[4]

Meanwhile, the fourth report, on the year 2001, states:

our numbers are based on a reporting system for
terminally-ill patients who legally receive prescriptions
for lethal medications, and do not include patients and
physicians who may act outside the law.[5]

These are odd statements for a state health authority to make. Why would a physician act outside the law when there is an established procedure for prescribing lethal drugs legally? We cannot know for sure, but the OHD must have written these disclaimers for some reason. One such reason may be that the physician wishes to meet the applicant's request in circumstances where the applicant does not fulfil all the criteria laid down by the ODDA. Such illegal acts would not necessarily be detected, as Oregon, unlike the UK, has no central prescriptions registry which could be expected to pick up illegal prescribing by physicians of lethal drugs. It is therefore impossible to say whether, and if so to what extent, action outside the law is taking place. All that can be said is that the official figures must show only a minimum figure for lethal prescriptions issued and assisted-suicide deaths taking place.

A further revealing detail of the Oregon figures is contained within the proportion of those receiving prescriptions for lethal drugs who had been referred by their assessing physician for psychiatric examination. Among the safeguards in the ODDA is the requirement that doctors ensure that there is no underlying depressive or mental condition suffered by those applying for an assisted suicide; they have to be of sound mind. The number of those who had been referred by their assessing physician for psychiatric examination has fallen steadily from 37 per cent when the ODDA was enacted to just 3 per cent in 2008 (the proportion actually hit 0 per cent in 2007, and was nil again in 2009). Now, it may be that those presenting themselves for state-sanctioned suicide may be growing progressively more sane. But the causes of this drop require further examination.

The OHD reports do not tell us how many applicants for assisted suicide were referred for psychiatric assessment and as a result rejected as suicide candidates. Such data would indeed be illuminating, throwing a light on the degree to which the psychiatry filter was working as intended. What they do tell us is how many of those who actually received prescriptions had been so referred as part of the assessment process and, by implication, declared sufficiently psychologically fit for purpose. One would expect there to be a margin of such cases; applicants whose psychological profile was not sufficiently clear to an assessing physician but who were confirmed to be of sound mind after examination by a psychiatric specialist. What is not clear is why there has been such a sharp fall in referrals of patients who, ultimately, get the green light. Two possible explanations present themselves.

First, we might assume that assessing physicians are becoming more adept at identifying any underlying psychological conditions among patients applying for an assisted suicide and are consequently not bothering a psychiatrist with a referral. Or, secondly, it might be that the physicians who are increasingly doing the assessments are those recommended by the pro-suicide organization Compassion and Choices and who are, for this reason, less inclined to see applications for assisted suicide as a sign of psychological imbalance. The President of Compassion and Choices told a British parliamentary select committee in 2004[6] that "over the last six years Compassion in Dying[7] has participated in a consultative way with about three quarters of the patients who have made a request under the Assisted Dying Act to take medication under the Act".[8] (Again, note that use of the word "medication", but let it pass.)

If the second of these propositions is plausible, as I believe it must be, then what has developed in Oregon is what is known on the circuit as "doctor shopping" – a tendency for patients to shop around for the treatment that they want, in this case an assisted suicide. We have already seen in Chapter 1 the effect that the triumph of consumerism might have had on a human psyche that has become accustomed to being offered choice in every aspect of their lives; the death we want simply becomes another consumer commodity. So it is with doctor shopping in Oregon. This is a disturbing outcome, implying that increasing numbers of applicants for assisted suicide are being assessed by physicians who may be less than coldly objective and independent in their patient assessments. What we are witnessing in Oregon – and would see in Britain, as well as other countries, if (or "when", as Dignity in Dying so complacently puts it) assisted suicide is legalized here – is the development of a two-tier health service in end-of-life care, in which there are doctors for assisted dying and doctors who assist with living, who may practise more consistently in the tradition of Hippocrates.

This crucial aspect to the debate over whether the ODDA operates as "successfully" as Dignity in Dying claims requires some forensic analysis of the OHD reports, to establish whether there is evidence of doctor-shopping. This evidence is likely to be found in the statistics for how many doctors the applicants for assisted suicide had to consult to receive the referral they sought and how many lethal prescriptions individual "death doctors" wrote. A key breakdown is as follows:

- In 1998, 6 of the 16 patients who chose physician-assisted suicide had to approach more than one physician before finding one who would start the prescription process.

- In 1999, 8 (31 per cent) out of 27 participating patients received a prescription from the first physician they asked. Of the remaining 18 participants (one had received their lethal dose in a previous year and ingested it during 1999), ten asked one other physician and eight asked two to three physicians.

- In 2000, 14 (56 per cent) out of 27 Oregonians who ended their lives via an assisted suicide did not receive a prescription from the first doctor approached.

- In 2004, of the 40 physicians who wrote prescriptions, 28 wrote one prescription, nine wrote two prescriptions, one wrote three prescriptions, another wrote four prescriptions, and one wrote seven prescriptions.

- In 2005, of the 39 physicians who wrote prescriptions, 29 wrote one prescription, three wrote two prescriptions, three wrote three prescriptions, three wrote four prescriptions and one wrote eight prescriptions. (From 2006 the OHD reports do not cover this issue.)

What is clear from this extrapolation is that a significant proportion of prescriptions are not being written by the first doctor approached. One might expect this doctor to be the physician most familiar with the patient's medical condition and state of mind. But many of Oregon's suicides are being assisted by further consultations with doctors whose knowledge of the patient is likely to be more partial. It is also clear that, while most doctors do this no more than once in a year, there is a hard core of physicians who do not see the writing of a prescription for lethal drugs as a one-off or rare event. That one doctor should feel able to write seven or eight such prescriptions, way ahead of colleagues, in a year is profoundly disturbing.

And so the question has to be asked: Are applicants for assisted suicide being connected with compliant doctors? And, if so, how? There is a potential link to be made between the issue of doctor-shopping and that of psychiatric assessment – or, as we have noted, the decreasing incidence of it. Part of the answer could lie in a facilitating role performed by the agency Compassion and Choices, an Oregon-based lobbyist and agent whose brief falls somewhere between Britain's Dignity in Dying and Switzerland's Dignitas clinic. There is no unambiguous evidence that Compassion and Choices is acting as a broker in this respect. While the organization admits that it has been "involved" in a majority of the assisted suicide deaths in Oregon to date, it does not state in so many words that this involvement has included connecting applicants with sympathetic doctors. Perhaps the best guide is that given by Ziegler and Bosshard in an article (published in February 2007 in the *British Medical Journal*) entitled "The Role of Non-Governmental Organisations in Physician Assisted Suicide". This article describes the role of Compassion and Choices as follows (my emphases):

Since physician assisted suicide is lawful in Oregon, the primary function of Compassion and Choices staff and volunteers in the state is directed *at ensuring access* and providing information as well as emotional support to patients and families. The law requires that two doctors are involved, one to prescribe and the other to consult. The organisation plays no part in assessing a patient's legal capacity since that responsibility rests with the doctor. Rather *it helps ensure access to assisted suicide* by discussing the eligibility process with interested parties and by *providing information and assurance to doctors who want to comply with the Oregon law* and qualify for its protections. However, some Oregon doctors are hesitant to assume the lead role of the prescribing physician and would rather be the consulting physician. In these cases *the organisation will suggest that the patient asks to be referred to another doctor who would consider being the prescribing physician.*

Apart from the agency role that is being played here by Compassion and Choices, it is also worth noting in passing the reference to "two doctors". Lord Falconer's defeated amendment to the Justice and Coroners Bill in the House of Lords in Britain, debated in July 2009, proposed that "prior to the act, two registered medical practitioners, independent of each other, have certified that they are of the opinion in good faith that [the person to be assisted in suicide] is terminally ill and has the capacity to make [a] declaration." The introduction of assisted suicide to the British legislature leans heavily on the Oregon model – indeed, as we have seen, Dignity in Dying is a big fan of the Oregon way of doing things. But the "two doctors" routine is clearly flawed, in that patients will shop around for a suicide-friendly doctor and because "some Oregon doctors are hesitant", according to the *BMJ*, an organization such as Compassion and Choices will intercede on their behalf. It's hard to discern an ideological difference between

Compassion and Choices in Oregon and Dignity in Dying in Britain, so Lord Falconer's "two doctors" fantasy and an agency function matching assisted-suicide applicants to sympathetic doctors looks like being the reality of an adoption of the Oregon model in Britain, whatever the claims made by its proponents for safeguards and regulation. We are entitled to ask whether we want to live in a society that resembles what Oregon really is, rather than the image that Oregon's apologists in the UK pretend is the reality.

Oregon: The vulnerable

It is a central tenet of faith in the case for assisted suicide that there are no "vulnerable groups", demographics in which assisted suicide might be disproportionately appealing as a way out of intolerable circumstances. This would be to concede that there is a type of person who is more likely to want to end his or her life, rather than terminally ill people from across the demographic scale. One category of humanity that the assisted-suicide lobby is particularly anxious not to have identified as particularly vulnerable to the introduction of the practice is the elderly. Any suggestion that society is developing a taste for culling its senior citizens, or encouraging them to relieve it of the burden of caring for them, or is developing a culture in which old age is valued less highly by that society, would be likely to turn public opinion strongly against the user-friendly image of the assisted-suicide and euthanasia industry. Enthusiasts for assisted suicide are consequently at pains to demonstrate that they are endeavouring to provide a death service for the terminally ill of all adult ages, not just for the elderly. Oregon tells a rather different story.

Among the ODDA's cheerleaders is Margaret Battin, of the Department of Philosophy at the University of Utah in Salt Lake City. In 2007 she published, along with others, a research paper (reproduced by the *British Medical Journal*) that purported to show that the Oregon ODDA did not put vulnerable groups at risk. Her thesis is flawed and obfuscates issues (one of her vulnerable groups is "the poor", while assisted suicide is actually more prevalent in the more affluent socio-demographic groups; if anything, "the wealthy" are a greater risk group). We are told by Battin that:

> in Oregon 10 per cent of patients who died by [assisted
> suicide] were 85 or older, whereas 21 per cent of all
> Oregon deaths were among persons in this age category.[9]

We are also told that:

> persons aged 18–64 years were over three times more
> likely than those over 85 years to receive assisted dying.[10]

The OHD report on the implementation of ODDA law in 2007 reveals that Battin and her fellow authors of the paper are quoting selectively in order to reach a predetermined conclusion. While the OHD report broadly corroborates the claims that over-85s are (somewhat unsurprisingly) twice as likely to die of natural causes as of assisted suicide and that the death rate from assisted suicide among 18–64 year-olds is three times as high as that among the over-85s, it also shows that 56 per cent of all assisted suicides occurred in the age group 65–84, compared with 35 per cent among those aged 18–64, and that the death rate from assisted suicides among people aged between 65 and 74 is actually higher than the death rate from other causes in this age group. What the OHD's figures in reality show, therefore, is that the greatest resort to assisted suicide in Oregon is in the 65–84 age group, with the 65–74 sub-group in particular being affected. Battin and her colleagues seek to define "elderly" as being over 85, where (again unsurprisingly) assisted suicide is relatively rare, nature taking its course more often than in other groups. Most reasonable people would accept that the elderly start at 65 (middle age has certainly ended by then), the current retirement age in the UK, which would make this group very much more vulnerable to assisted suicide. For Battin to conclude in the light of this that there is "no evidence of heightened risk" among the elderly is nothing short of perverse. This category of people, who are very much at issue in any examination of vulnerability to legalized assisted dying, are clearly at risk. (Stop Press: The median age for those who died by assisted suicide in Oregon in 2009 was 76 and the most common age group was 75–84. The pattern for assisted suicide being a practice for the elderly is becoming well established, so Battin's contention is just plain wrong.)

As for the reasons given for seeking an assisted suicide, the OHD figures show little variation from year to year. The top three reasons listed were "loss of autonomy due to illness", "loss of control of bodily functions" and "inability to participate in enjoyable activities". More worryingly, the numbers who listed inadequate pain control, being a burden on friends and family and inability to afford health care, though small, show a rising trend. These figures – and the issues they reflect – require some unpacking.

But, first, it's worth noting that these principal reasons accord with evidence given to Lord Mackay's House of Lords select committee in December 2004. The committee was told then that candidates for assisted suicide tended to be

> pragmatic, matter-of-fact persons who have always been in control of their lives and want control... They want control of their dying process and want to avert having to be cared for in a way that is offensive to them... It is crystal clear to them that they want to name the day, and when they are finished, when life has served them and enough is enough, they are done.[11]

The committee was also told:

> Most folks said they find being cared for to be intolerable and they have had a lifetime of needing to be responsible and have learned, one way or another, to be self sufficient.[12]

Not much evidence here of the intolerable pain of terminal illness that UK proponents of the legalization of assisted suicide, such as Lord Falconer and Dignity in Dying, tend to talk about. It's also true that, while singing the praises of the Oregon system, proponents of assisted suicide in the UK become very po-faced about assisted suicide only being available for the terminally ill. Where exactly do the "inability to participate in enjoyable activities" or "control over [the] dying process" as reasons for assisted suicide fit into their appreciation for Oregon's practices? Is this what the UK lobby wants to see as common UK practice, just as soon as it has got assisted suicide for the terminally ill, suffering intolerable pain, legalized? That's some slippery slope.

A number of crucial issues arise out of these real, American reasons given for assisted suicide that are recorded in the OHD reports. The first and clearest point is that the heavy emphasis on loss of autonomy, inability to enjoy life and loss of bodily function suggests that assisted suicide is being seen less as a means of relieving intolerable symptomatic suffering and more as a means of being in personal control over the dying process. Again, this perspective needs to be highlighted in order to counter the pro-euthanasia movement's line that assisted-dying legislation is necessary in order to provide an escape from pain and other severe symptomatic distress. No one should seek to underestimate the real suffering behind the reasons that really are cited for wanting assisted suicide, but pain does not, in reality, rank high in the list of Oregonians' reasons for opting for assisted suicide.

While the OHD report does list "inadequate pain control" as a reason for applying for assisted suicide, the term is intended to cover both concern about actual pain and fear of intractable pain in the future. While the number of applicants listing this as a reason for assisted suicide was low at the outset, it has risen steadily over the past eleven years to a peak in 2006, in which year nearly half of those who took their own lives via assisted suicide listed inadequate pain control as a reason. The number has fallen back again in 2008, but it remains to be seen whether the upward trend will be resumed. Whether or not that happens, the overall trend of patients listing inadequate pain control as a reason for opting for assisted suicide is hard to reconcile with claims from its supporters that since enactment of the ODDA, palliative care in Oregon has improved.

Similarly and shockingly, the number of applicants for assisted suicide listing "not wanting to be a burden on family, friends and caregivers" has also risen steadily since the ODDA came into force. In 1998, this was given as a reason by only one in eight of those who died by assisted suicide, whereas in 2008 one third of those who took their lives listed this as a reason. Noting the start of this upward trend, the OHD report for 2000 observed:

> That Oregon [assisted suicide] patients almost always
> discussed concern about becoming a burden in
> conjunction with losing autonomy suggests that it might
> be part of patients' ideas about independence. However,
> a negative interpretation of concern about becoming a
> burden is that patients may feel pressured by others into
> using [assisted suicide].[13]

Although the report goes on to add that "no evidence indicates that such pressure has been a primary motivating influence among the 70 Oregon patients participating to date", it is difficult to see how such evidence could come to light. We have here a grotesque situation that has developed in Oregon, with the implication that a non-dependency culture could be growing among the terminally ill and their relatives, where those relatives are bringing pressure on patients to go for an assisted suicide, consciously or otherwise. That is very much part of the assisted-suicide package that British supporters of the Oregon model would import – again, consciously or otherwise.

Oregon: The devil in the detail

The bureaucracy of taking your own life in Oregon and the light-touch regulation of the procedures serve further to undermine the proposal that it offers us a model to emulate. The form that applicants for assisted suicide are required to complete includes the declaration that "I make this request voluntarily and without reservation". The witnesses to the signing of the form are meanwhile asked to state that the applicant "appears to be of sound mind and not under duress, fraud or undue influence". This echoes the Director of Public Prosecutions' guidelines for potentially non-prosecutable assisted suicide, announced in the UK in 2010, and is obviously meant to ensure that the patient is acting under his or her own volition and is not being coerced or manipulated into suicide. But there is, startlingly, no procedure for confirming that this situation obtains at the time the lethal drugs are ingested. Note that many of those who receive prescriptions for lethal drugs do not take the drugs until some time after their receipt. The OHD's report on the year 2004 records the mean interval between first request and death as 33 days, with a range of 15 to 593 days. It's clearly possible that, in the intervening period, patients could become depressed or be subjected to duress, however subtle, from relatives to end their lives, or indeed undergo a change of mind. Moreover, there is no requirement for the prescribing physician to be present when the lethal drugs are ingested; in practice, few of them are present (a doctor was present, for instance, at just 23 per cent of deaths, according to the OHD's report on 2005). The act of killing is usually called physician-assisted suicide (or PAS), which rather implies that the doctor assists with the act of self-destruction, but the reality is that they usually absent themselves from that, having simply given the clearance for the suicide to occur and provided the means to do it. In another walk of life, this would surely be seen as an abrogation of pastoral care.

The patient's initial assessment may very well be made with neutral professional integrity (though, as we have seen, doctor-shopping rather erodes this claim), but there is no way of confirming that, at the time when applicants actually take the lethal drugs, they are of sound mind, are acting on their own volition and without reservation and are not under duress or undue influence from others. Nor, as there is not a requirement for the death to be witnessed by a disinterested party, is there any way of knowing whether the drugs are self-administered or administered by others. It is interesting in this context to note that the ODDA does not refer to self-administration of the drugs but simply to the "act of ingesting", which could include administration by others as well as by the patient.

Indeed, it is fair to say that patients who have been assessed as suitable for assisted suicide and have taken possession of lethal drugs have placed themselves at risk of pressure or abuse by others. It would not be difficult for someone with malicious intent surreptitiously to mix the lethal drugs into normal food, to present them in this form to the person concerned and to claim plausibly after the death that they had been self-administered as an act of legal assisted suicide. It is all too easy to say that there is no evidence of foul play. But how would such evidence ever arise? And it's difficult to know how this unsatisfactory practice could be improved under any other jurisdiction. Either we would have to insist that the suicide occurred immediately after the initial assessment, which would be peremptory and allow no "cooling-off period"; or the patient would have to be re-assessed just ahead of the suicide, which would have the unfortunate effect of putting a date on the suicide, with its attendant coercive pressures. Yet, disturbingly, I have participated in a debate in the UK at which those speaking in favour of assisted suicide, Professor Paul Badham, a patron of Dignity in Dying, and the Liberal Democrat MP for Romsey, Sandra Gidley, have asserted enthusiastically that the distribution of lethal drugs on the Oregon model, to be ingested at any time in the future, is the best procedure to be adopted in Britain.

Oregon's regulatory code for assisted suicide is similarly unsatisfactory. The OHD set out its responsibilities for monitoring and regulation in a report published shortly after the ODDA came into force.[14] It is clear from this report, and from the annual reports issued on the working of the ODDA, that the OHD operates a hands-off system of regulation. In particular:

- There is no post-event examination of assisted suicide cases along the lines of the Regional Assessment Committees that exist in the Netherlands. Once a doctor has written a lethal prescription and submitted the necessary paperwork to the OHDS, the case is at an end.

- Oregon does not have a central prescriptions registry which could detect illegal prescribing of lethal drugs. It is impossible to say whether such illicit prescription occurs, but in its 1999 report the OHD felt it necessary to "remind all our physician readers that prescriptions written under the Death with Dignity Act must be reported".

- There have been a number of worrying stories reported by Oregon-based groups opposed to the ODDA, including that of Kate Cheney, an elderly woman suffering from dementia and terminal cancer who was refused an assisted suicide by several doctors before obtaining a lethal prescription from a more compliant physician. It is not known whether these cases have been officially investigated and, if so, with what result. The evidence provided seems to rest largely on newspaper reports. What is clear, however, is that the OHD appears to have a relationship of trust with physicians who practise assisted suicide. Its 1999 report, commenting on the accounts given by doctors of cases in which they had written prescriptions under the ODDA, states that their entire testimony could have amounted to "a cock-and-bull story. We assume, however, that physicians were their usual careful and accurate selves".

- The OHD admits in its 1999 report that it "has no formal enforcement role". It continues that "we are required to report any non-compliance with the law to the Oregon Board of Medical Examiners for further investigation", but adds, somewhat cryptically, that "because of this obligation, we cannot detect or accurately comment on issues that may be under reported". What this appears to mean, in plain language, is that the OHD can investigate what is reported to it by prescribing physicians but has no knowledge of what is not reported.

It is, of course, entirely credible that another legislature could seek to introduce tighter regulation and accountability for assisted suicide. But the Oregon experience demonstrates that it is fraught with difficulties. And, meanwhile, the Oregon model is held up as a paradigm of best practice by those who would have assisted suicide legalized in Britain. Oregon is very far from being that.

The inadequacies of the Oregon model can be summarized as follows:

- The apparently low number of assisted-suicide cases in Oregon (60 in 2008) needs to be put into context. The same incidence of assisted suicide would produce nearly 1,000 cases annually in the UK.

- The number of Oregon cases is now nearly four times the number when the Act first came into operation.

- The number of successful applications in which a prior referral for psychiatric assessment was made has fallen from more than one in three to almost none by 2008.

- A significant proportion of prescriptions are being written not by the first doctor approached, whom one would expect to be the physician most familiar with the patient's medical condition, but by another doctor, whose knowledge of the patient is likely to be weaker.

- It is also clear that many of those who receive prescriptions for lethal drugs are being connected with willing physicians by the organization Compassion and Choices, and the suspicion must remain therefore that the assessments being given are in some cases less than entirely objective.

- These factors, taken together, may serve to explain research findings, published in the *BMJ* in the autumn of 2008, that one in four of a sample of assisted-suicide cases revealed the presence of undiagnosed depression.

- Contrary to the claims of pro-ODDA advocates, the main incidence of assisted suicide in Oregon is among the elderly.

- It is clear from the reasons given by applicants seeking assisted suicide that there is a growing incidence of concern over poor pain relief, which is inconsistent with claims that palliative care in Oregon has improved since the ODDA was enacted, and over fears of being a burden on others, which points to a growing presence of internalized pressures and/or coercion for assisted suicide.

- The application system for assisted suicide in Oregon contains few safeguards to protect the vulnerable. This is particularly so for patients who have completed the assessment process and received their prescribed lethal drugs. There is no mechanism to confirm their state of mind, willingness or freedom from duress at the time of the ingestion of the lethal drugs, or even to ensure that the drugs are self-administered.

- Regulation of the ODDA is near to non-existent. There is no system of rigorous post-event scrutiny of assisted-suicide cases, and the Oregon Health Department openly admits that its reports on the working of the Act are based on the good faith of reporting doctors. There is no central prescriptions registry which might be able to detect prescription that is outside the law.

The Dutch experience

There is no need to rehearse those areas in which another jurisdiction echoes the experience of assisted suicide in Oregon. Doctor-shopping, the dark and subtle processes of coercion, and lifestyle decisions for assisted suicide are likely to crop up to some degree or another wherever the option is available in law. But, as the Parliamentary Select Committee on Assisted Dying report for Lord Joffe's Bill in 2005 makes abundantly clear, the history of assisted suicide and voluntary euthanasia in the Netherlands is very different from that in Oregon and throws up some separate issues that need to be addressed in any assessment of whether assisted suicide is something that could be tolerated in the UK legislature. First, we need a brief description of where the Dutch stand on end-of-life provision.

Though a law legalizing assisted-suicide practices was only passed by the Dutch parliament in 2002, the criminal and supreme courts of the country had since 1973 adjudicated on a number of cases where defendants had invoked – invariably successfully – the defence of necessity against a charge of murder. The motivation for the Dutch legislature was not dissimilar from that of the UK Law Lords in 2009, who directed that the Director of Public Prosecutions must clarify when those who assisted a suicide would be prosecuted, specifically in response to the Debbie Purdy case, but also against the background of Britons assisting with suicides in Switzerland and escaping prosecution. In Holland, the 2002 Act was similarly a codification of existing practices which had been built up on a basis of case law. The purpose of moving from case law to statute law was to remove the uncertainties, for doctors and patients, which had surrounded earlier adjudication of cases brought before the courts.

There is a key difference between the 2002 Dutch law and the 1997 law in Oregon: Dutch law permits voluntary euthanasia as well as assisted suicide. Euthanasia is defined in Holland in a highly specific way. In Dutch law, the term "euthanasia" includes what is more widely known as "assisted suicide". On the other hand, it specifically excludes the ending of a person's life without his or her request. In other words, the Dutch do not recognize the existence of involuntary as well as voluntary euthanasia: while the latter is now permissible in law, the former is still regarded as murder – though as we shall see, that interpretation is malleable.

The 2002 law is not limited to adults. Nor does an applicant for euthanasia have to be terminally ill. The principal criterion is "hopeless and unbearable suffering". It has nothing to do with life expectancy. Five regional assessment committees, set up under the 2002 law, monitor the criteria for Dutch euthanasia. But, like Oregon, they are light of touch. The committees do not have a role in monitoring euthanasia practices and there is no routine procedure which would show whether some physicians are performing significantly more euthanasias than others, which would demonstrate the kind of two-tier structure in which people "shop" for death in Oregon.

Approximately 16 million people live in the Netherlands, of whom around 140,000 die every year. The 2005 British parliamentary inquiry found that some 9,700 requests for euthanasia are made annually. About 3,800 of these actually receive euthanasia, of which some 300 are assisted suicides. Euthanasia therefore accounts for around 2.5 per cent and assisted suicide 0.2 per cent of all deaths in the Netherlands. Crucially, in addition to these, there are about 1,000 deaths a year (0.7 per cent of all deaths) where physicians end a patient's life without an explicit request at the time of death, despite the formal illegality to which I refer above. Sometimes this will be because the original requests have been made some time, occasionally years, before the actual date of the euthanasia, but objective judgments are clearly also being made as to whether a living human being's life is worth preserving. This is a truly sinister development that goes to the heart of the issue of whether assisted suicide and/or euthanasia could ever be acceptable in Britain or elsewhere. Those who support its prospect in the UK will always claim that it can only be countenanced for those who are terminally ill and have requested it and that the system works well abroad. The experience in Holland doesn't support that claim.

Holland: Killing the imperfect

How do around 1,000 people come to be put to death in Holland per year without having made a request to die? At the 2005 parliamentary select committee, Dr Johann Legemaate of the Royal Dutch Medical Association said: "this happens mostly with patients suffering from cancer in the last days or hours of their life." That is, perhaps, worrying enough; Dutch doctors' opinions of when it is appropriate to dispatch a patient are likely to vary wildly. But Dr Ruben van Coevorden introduced an even darker attitude:

> It involves ending life without request, but it is outside
> the scope of this discussion because it involves newborn
> children, with defects and so on.[15]

This view was echoed by Jacob Kohnstamm, Chairman of NVVE, which is the Dutch arm of the World Federation of Right to Die Societies, of which, of course, the British Dignity in Dying is also a member:

> they are, for example, in neonatology, severely
> handicapped new-born babies – problems that are mainly
> in the medical sphere.[16]

And this from Irene Keizer, a senior policy officer at the Dutch Ministry of Health:

> There are some cases in which it is not careful euthanasia,
> but in most cases are people who are not able to make
> a request because they are not seen as able to make a
> request – for instance, people who are suffering from a
> psychiatric disease or people who are in a coma. Also
> newborn babies are not capable of making a request.[17]

Newborn babies are indeed incapable of making a request. And the implications of that remark need no further amplification here.

When asked what proportions of the total might consist of people in these various categories, Ms Keizer thought that about half of them were people not capable of making a request (e.g. they were in a coma), while "25 per cent are people who could have made a request but did not, so we are wondering about those, 15 per cent are newborn babies, and 10 per cent are other categories." We might wonder what the Dutch government will do when it has finished "wondering about those". But the signs are that, like Switzerland, Holland is regretting the haste with which it introduced assisted-suicide legislation. Dr Els Borst, the former Health Minister and Deputy Prime Minister who guided the law through the Dutch parliament, now says it was brought in "far too early". Without elaborating, she admitted that medical care for the terminally ill had declined since the law came into effect. She said more should have been done legally to protect people who wanted to die natural deaths.[18]

Meanwhile we should satisfy ourselves with the knowledge that, even in a highly developed medical service in an advanced Western, democratic nation such as Holland, the introduction of euthanasia has led ineluctably to a circumstance in which an official can talk easily and procedurally about the destruction of newborn babies, while some 35 per cent of those human beings who were killed without a request for euthanasia fall into the vague categories of being "wondered about" or are unspecified "other categories". As Professor Gerrit van der Wal, head of the department of Public Health at the EMGO Institute in Amsterdam, put it:

> As we also know from qualitative studies, doctors feel
> that they have their back against the wall; that the family
> and nurses are asking him or her to end this suffering
> and this unbearable state of life; and then they decide to
> hasten the end of life. Whether or not this is very explicit
> is not that clear... We are neutral researchers, but we do
> not like these cases... We hoped that they would decrease
> in number, but it has not happened.[19]

Enthusiasts for the introduction of euthanasia into the UK are keen to suggest that a legalized and strictly controlled system provides safeguards that make for fewer cases of unsolicited euthanasia than occur where no such supervision is in place. Holland's experience contradicts that. Professor van der Wal tellingly added to his submission:

"So far as we can see, there is no association between the development in jurisprudence and law and life-ending cases without a request."

Holland: Hidden euthanasia

And that's before we get to this worrying Dutch statistic: it is estimated (a figure accepted by the 2005 select committee) that just *54 per cent* of all euthanasias in the Netherlands are reported to the authorities. Despite all claims by British euthanasia lobbyists that transparency is enhanced in countries with legalized systems of assisted dying, hidden euthanasia remains a critical problem in Holland. This is especially curious, given that one of the conditions of immunity from prosecution under the 2002 law is that all cases of euthanasia are reported. At the time of the 2005 inquiry, Dr Bregje Onwuteaka-Philipsen, an associate professor at the Free University of Amsterdam, believed there were three reasons:

> There are people who still do not want the administrative bother of it, or the idea that you report it. There are people who think that you should not report it, either because they feel that it is not really euthanasia or because it is something between the doctor and the patient. It is also possible that there are people who perhaps doubt whether the case would go through easily – whether they have exactly fulfilled all the requirements.[20]

Even where euthanasia is legal, it seems that there are reasons for concealing it. Ethical and moral issues are not simply dealt with in a legislature and there is some evidence that doctors remain ashamed of euthanasia, even where it is sanctioned by the state. Or it may be that unscrupulous doctors feel encouraged to test the ethical boundaries in jurisdictions which have already become morally compromised through the abandonment of the moral high ground, where the immutable commitment is only to the preservation of human life and the relief of pain.

Holland: The decline of palliative care

We need to examine the state of palliative care in the Netherlands and its relationship with euthanasia. There has been a substantial investment in palliative care in Holland in recent decades, as a result of which palliative care departments and regional specialist teams had been created throughout the country. And more resources have been devoted to raising palliative care standards in nursing homes and care homes.

However, the approach is now generalist; this means that all GPs and nurses must have been trained to give palliative care. So palliative care is not now recognized in the Netherlands as a clinical specialism. Significantly, this generalist-only approach has been adopted because most people in Holland die at home; hospitals are now largely devoid of input from palliative-care specialists. On the one hand, this development has had the happy effect of meaning that many GPs, knowing the basics of palliative care, can confidently resist the pressure from the family if they can offer something instead of euthanasia. And palliative care in hospices is excellent; figures show that patients entering hospices who request euthanasia have increasingly withdrawn those requests when palliative care is provided. That is telling in that sufficient and satisfactory palliative care is clearly, for many, a preferable substitute for euthanasia.

But all is not as it seems. Dutch doctors report that, whereas there had been an increase in funding for palliative care in the late 1990s to accompany discussion in parliament of euthanasia legislation, that funding has now ceased. And the funding which has taken place has produced a growth in the quantity, but not necessarily the quality, of palliative care. Since there was much investment at the end of the 1990s and the beginning of the new century, institutions which were providing nursing care in general were opening palliative care units, because they received more money for the patients. The number of palliative care units in Holland has consequently increased considerably, but these people are mostly just continuing what they were doing, in the sense that there is no real specialist understanding, knowledge and practice of palliative care. So the number of places where palliative care is offered does not say very much about the quality of palliative care in general in the Netherlands.

The truth is that where palliative care has maintained a high level of specialist excellence, euthanasia has withered as an option. Take St Jacob's Hospice in Amsterdam. It has wards for medical and psycho-geriatric care and for rehabilitation, plus a stroke unit. And in the late 1990s it opened a palliative care unit. So St Jacob's provides a hospice facility within a broader establishment for care of the elderly. And, although St Jacob's has grown out of a Christian foundation, it has not set its face against euthanasia. But it is rarely asked for. The reason for this is that the quality of palliative care in such nursing homes is relatively high, compared with GPs and other health officials who have simply been on a palliative course. Furthermore, according to Dr Roeli Dijkman, President of the Dutch Society of Nursing Home Physicians:

> patients who suffer from terminal illnesses make the
> request for euthanasia before they go to the nursing
> home. In principle, the patients who ask for euthanasia
> have a vision of dying and losing their dignity... when
> you have a terminal illness at home and you do not want
> to die by fading away with palliative care, you decide to
> have euthanasia at home. Most euthanasias are by general
> practitioners.[21]

Ironically enough, Holland turns out to be less of an advertisement for the efficacy of euthanasia than one for proper, professional and effective investment in and implementation of palliative care. Repeatedly, in an analysis of the choices offered to societies in end-of-life provision, we garner evidence that investment of energy and resources in palliative care trumps simply assisting the dying to die.

Among the "euthanasia statements" that the NVVE, Holland's opposite number to the UK's Dignity in Dying, has offered its members is the following little counsel of despair: Applicants are invited to opt for euthanasia as and when it is "virtually impossible for me to perform what are for me worthwhile activities such as reading, writing, watching television, listening to music and doing manual work or handicrafts". This forms part of an exercise for deciding when life has become "unbearable". Palliative-care specialists may reasonably counter that it is well within the provision of their skills to ensure that life is still joyful and fulfilling for those who have lost the ability to watch television or perform macramé. That this should be a yardstick for deciding whether to kill yourself would be laughable if it were not so tragic. But this is where euthanasia can take us. No wonder a sizeable proportion of Dutch doctors resist it. And, significantly, they are informed in their opposition by their faith.

According to Dr Legemaate, some "20–25 per cent… are opposed, mostly for religious reasons and also on some non-religious reasons – for instance, that it is not compatible with their medical oath or the medical profession." How an incompatibility with a medical oath can be conceived as a "non-religious reason" is a moot point. Dr Legemaate adds in select-committee evidence: "There has been a kind of increasing acceptance of doing euthanasia, which I think incorporates a certain change of opinion about the moral aspects and how you balance that."

That would seem to imply that, as in Oregon, not only is a two-tier medical service emerging in Holland, with one fifth to a quarter continuing to be committed to a Hippocratic code of the primacy of human life with palliative care, and the majority now adopting a more negative-utilitarian or existential attitude. According to Dr Maria van den Muijsenburgh's own research, while Dutch doctors were willing and capable of administering intense and very personal palliative care that met the needs of their patients, there was a considerable variation among physicians with regard to the incidence of euthanasia. While most doctors, she said, were supportive of their patients, "there were... doctors who were very willing to commit euthanasia – doctors who themselves thought 'suffering is useless' – and more than half of their patients die by euthanasia."

Welcome to a medical profession that has allowed its ethos to be undermined by an acceptance of death as a medical "treatment", over the age-old respect for the sanctity of human life.

The Switzerland experience

Switzerland is best known in Britain as a destination for assisted dying and Zurich has become the European capital for "death tourism", a title that it has become anxious to shed, as we shall see. It is closer in its practice to Oregon than Holland, but Switzerland's practices are again different. Under Swiss law, voluntary euthanasia is illegal, but assisted suicide is permissible, so long as such assistance is provided for honourable motives, such as to relieve suffering. The situation in Switzerland differs also from the position in Oregon and the Netherlands in that assistance with suicide is not regarded as the exclusive province of doctors. Where lethal medication is required, a doctor's prescription is needed for this to be obtained, though this requirement exists in order to ensure control of dangerous drugs and not because of a view that assistance with suicide is a function of medicine.

A further difference in the Swiss situation is the involvement of voluntary organizations. The most famous, though rapidly becoming the most notorious, is Dignitas, which is a breakaway group from another death-tourism agency, Exit. The active help which such organizations provide to applicants, including medical examinations and facilities for suicide to take place, is the principal distinguishing feature of assisted suicide in Switzerland.

The Swiss government has grown increasingly concerned about

its role in European suicide and, at the very moment that Britain was effectively making assisted suicide simpler for its citizens, through the Director of Public Prosecutions' "clarification" in 2009 of when those who assisted in a suicide would not face prosecution, Switzerland has been moving to make the process more difficult. Far from being the kind of relaxed and unremarkable service that its proponents would have us believe it is, assisted suicide in Switzerland has become an uncharacteristically sordid and shaming aspect of Swiss society.

Dignitas was founded in 1998 and, even by 2005, Swiss officials were expressing concerns about the country's role in assisted death. Dr Andreas Brunner, Attorney-General of the Canton of Zurich, told the 2005 UK parliamentary select committee that he was concerned about circumstances where "a person comes today and dies the same day", which is common Dignitas practice, since this inevitably precluded the building up of a proper relationship between a terminally ill patient who is assisted to take his or her own life and the doctor who assesses the case. There have been a number of proposals put forward in the Swiss Parliament to combat such "death tourism". Bernardo Stadelmann of the Federal Ministry of Justice told the committee that the Swiss authorities were aware of the problem and that the government was trying "to ascertain whether there is a danger of the situation in Switzerland being exploited and, if so, [it would] take appropriate steps to remedy the situation". More recently, Eveline Widmer Schlumpf, the Swiss justice minister, has become concerned that the Swiss law on assisted suicide should be tightened to avoid abuse and to protect Switzerland's reputation. At least two of her colleagues in the Swiss cabinet are said to believe that assisted suicide should be outlawed altogether, to bring greater clarity and accountability to this largely unregulated area of medical practice.

The embarrassment caused to Switzerland by having Dignitas in Zurich is palpable. Dignitas is regularly called a "clinic" in the media. In reality it has operated from a series of ordinary rented apartments. These have become increasingly difficult for the organization to find. In 2007, *The Independent* reported in 2009, Dignitas was required to leave the Zurich apartment it had rented for its patients after local residents complained about the number of coffins entering and leaving the building. Subsequently, Dignitas assisted its clients to commit suicide in hotels, "prompting at least one hotelier to launch a legal action". Also in 2007, it was revealed that two Germans had killed themselves, with the help of Dignitas, in cars parked in motorway lay-bys on the outskirts of Zurich. For several months in 2008, Dignitas rented rooms in an industrial estate. Whatever claims are made for Dignitas – and it is the aim of assisted-suicide lobbyists to get the practice legalized in the UK so that Britons don't have to fly to Switzerland for this drab and humiliating end – "dignity in dying" is not an apt description of its activities.

Ludwig Minelli founded Dignitas in 1998. He told the 2005 inquiry that he would like to be able to help mentally ill people to commit suicide. Switzerland has a complex legal heritage of federal *cantons* and Minelli indicated that it was only some legal concerns that were holding Dignitas back from assisting the suicides of the mentally ill:

> Until now, we have been very reluctant to have mentally ill people because there is one procedure in the Canton of Aargau where this question has been raised. We had last week a hearing at the court... I think we will have more possibilities to help mentally ill people.[22]

Minelli has an enthusiasm for suicide which borders on the evangelistic. In a rare interview in September 2009, reported in the *Daily Telegraph*, he said:

> It's a right, a human right, without condition except capacity for discernment. I have a totally different attitude to suicide. I say suicide is a marvellous possibility given to a human being. Suicide is a very good possibility to escape a situation which you can't alter. It is not a condition to have a terminal illness. Terminal illness is a British obsession.[23]

So, in Minelli's world, suicide can be a permanent solution to a temporary problem. He went on to give a specific example of where he would like to see his suicide service being delivered:

> There is a couple living in Canada. The husband is ill; his partner is not ill but she told us… "if my husband goes, I would go at the same time with him"… we will probably now go to the courts in order to clear this question.[24]

Given this transatlantic reach for Dignitas, plus more than 115 Britons who have used the Swiss operation to end their lives, Minelli's service is effectively operating in foreign jurisdictions. And, as a form of suicide-on-demand, we don't have to go as far as Canada to discover the Dignitas fate of those without terminal illnesses who wish to end their lives there. Two of the most high-profile assisted suicides performed through Dignitas for Britons are as follows:

- Daniel James, a 23-year-old paralysed from the neck down in a rugby accident, was taken by his parents to die at Dignitas in 2008.

- Sir Edward Downes, 85, and his wife, Joan, 74, died at Dignitas, their two children in attendance, in 2009. Lady Joan was suffering with cancer, though it is unclear what was her likely prognosis. Sir Edward, meanwhile, was visually impaired and had lost his hearing, a terrible affliction for a conductor emeritus with the BBC Philharmonic and reminiscent of Beethoven's fate, but he was not terminally ill.

Swiss concerns were expressed about Dignitas' remit and practices at the 2005 inquiry. Dr Christoph Rehmann-Sutter, president of the National Advisory Commission on Biomedical Ethics, referred to "the impossibility of the state having legal oversight of the practice of the organisations [such as Dignitas]". He added that they "do not put enough weight on the lengthy process of evaluation and assessment of the person or on giving support to the person to make him or her change their mind", reflecting the same-day service that many suicides receive.

Meanwhile, Dr Brunner (of the Zurich Canton) believed that Swiss suicide organizations should be more tightly regulated by the authorities: "There is no surveillance; they are associations without any state control. I think that should change." He claimed that a number of additional duties should be placed on organizations such as Dignitas, to allow the authorities to regulate them more effectively. For example, while the organizations already publish annual reports of their activities, Dr Brunner felt that they should be legally required to disclose all their accounts as well, thereby making it easier for the authorities to satisfy themselves that no financial profit was being derived from assistance with suicide, a key consideration given the insistence of Swiss law on non-self-serving motives. Dignitas' own bookkeeping has come in for official scrutiny; early in 2009, the Zurich public prosecutor's office called for more transparency from Dignitas, saying it remained unclear exactly what the organization's patient fee of approximately £6,000 was being spent on. Subsequent indications from Switzerland have suggested that monies invested in "right to die" campaigning abroad could breach the requirement that no one should benefit in kind from assisted suicides in Switzerland.

Dr Brunner added that he felt also that it was important to ensure that organizations such as Dignitas were staffed by "a good approved selection of people... because there is a danger from so-called angels of death". There is strong evidence over the past five years that the Swiss authorities want to clean up their country's provision of assisted suicides to foreigners. There is less evidence that Dignitas wants to change its ways. Indeed, events in the intervening period have tended to suggest that it wishes to relax its requirements further.

Conclusions

What are we to make of the state-approved practices of suicide in Oregon, Holland and Switzerland? It seems to me that there are two important conclusions that we can draw. One is secular, to which perhaps we can all relate, and the second is religious, arising from a Christian worldview, but I hope sufficiently integrated with and grounded in what flows from the secular issue to enable it to be addressed by anyone, and not just those who profess the Christian faith.

The first, secular point is to raise the question whether the introduction of assisted suicide and/or voluntary euthanasia in Britain would replicate the experience of Oregon, Holland or Switzerland. Proponents of its introduction to the UK legislature often speak of their concern for the terminally ill (though, as we have seen, they are far from always terminally ill) having to travel abroad, usually to Switzerland, to end their lives. They argue, as I have heard Dignity in Dying and Lord Falconer argue in debate with me on radio, that a system that was regulated in British law would be safer and more accountable for our citizens, with greater safeguards to ensure the probity of the process, than the situation at present that requires them to travel abroad to die at the time of their choosing. They will add that a carefully constructed system in the British legislature would have the added benefit of not requiring terminally ill people to travel abroad prematurely, for fear that they may become incapable of travelling later on and therefore unable to take their own lives (this was a central plank of multiple sclerosis sufferer Debbie Purdy's successful appeal for clarification of the law to the Law Lords in 2009). Permeating this belief is the implication that we in Britain could do so much better than foreign jurisdictions in the implementation of assisted suicide and euthanasia, that it would be firmly within the control of a nicer bunch of people than you find abroad and, in contrast to the mistakes and shortcomings of foreign legislatures, our own parliament could implement a system that only dispatched our terminally ill in joyful and universally fulfilling circumstances in which everyone's a winner.

But are the State of Oregon, Holland and Switzerland not sophisticated and fully developed Western societies, secular democracies in which the rule of law and moral imperatives enjoy dominion? It is beyond doubt that this federal state within the US and two sovereign nations within the European Union could harvest testimonials from families who will confirm that their "loved ones" died peacefully and appropriately in beautiful surroundings at the time of their own choosing (though we have yet to receive such an encomium from the deceased). I have not, it is true, trawled the thank-you letters of next of kin to demonstrate how those who are left behind think that assisted suicide in these places is a wonderful service that has served their families well. But consider Oregon's doctor-shopping and lack of knowledge about how and when its prescribed lethal prescriptions will be ingested, Holland's re-invention of palliative care as a generalist nursing function, and the squalid nature of some of Switzerland's suicides among those who simply say they want to die – are these things not a profound warning to the rest of us? I have gone into such detail about assisted suicides in these places because they are warnings of where we are headed if we adopt such practices in our legislature – and the creeping legislation has already begun with the Director of Public Prosecutions, outside the parliamentary legislative process, producing a checklist, however he may describe it differently, to avoid prosecution for assisting a suicide in Britain. Look at the health-service shortcomings and the moral compromise of places such as Oregon, Holland and Switzerland. They hold up a mirror to us, to show us ourselves and where we are headed. Is that really where we want to go, a world in which we prescribe the equivalent of Socrates' hemlock to those who say they want it, while letting our capacity for palliative care turn into something resembling an inferior accessory? Is that the world we want to live in? I suggest not.

Which brings us to the second conclusion. The practice of the Christian faith is one in which we speak of the Kingdom of Heaven, or the Kingdom of God. This is not, as some who are not of this faith suppose, some abstract heaven where the spirit of the good go for all eternity when they die. It is axiomatic that this Kingdom is meant to be built here in the world, a doctrine that is common to the three monotheistic, Abrahamic faiths of Judaism, Christianity and Islam.

For the Christian, the New Testament is littered with such references, but perhaps one of the most trenchant is from the Gospels, from the ministry of Jesus of Nazareth:

> The kingdom of God does not come with observation;
> nor will they say, "See here!" or "See there!" For indeed,
> the Kingdom of God is within you.
>
> (LUKE 17:20–21 NKJV)

Scholarly consensus hardens around a better translation being "the kingdom of God is among you". In short, Christians are enjoined to discover the Kingdom (a somewhat unsatisfactorily patriarchal word for our times) in their lives in the here and now and to help to build it. This isn't a concept that is confined to Christianity; it is familiar to anyone who takes a meta-narrative view of human history, a worldview that the human story is bound for a better, if not perfect, destination. There are plenty of utopian political creeds that have nothing to do with faith in God. This is a human journey to which neo-Marxists can relate. And, again, for those of us who believe that there is a higher purpose than the material to human existence, we need to repeat the question. Is the way in which places such as Oregon, Holland and Switzerland approach the disposal of human life something that serves a greater human purpose? Christians may speak of Kingdom values, though secularists will talk of civilized values and the world we wish to build. Even the great quantum physicist Professor Stephen Hawking, whose suffering of devastating Motor Neurone Disease must have taken him to the gates of euthanasia, can speak of "understanding the mind of God". Again, in these contexts, we are entitled to ask whether the places in the world that practise assisted suicide and euthanasia represent the kind of world in which we want to live and die. Or whether, in contrast, they call us to find something better, a world in which we aspire to nurture and cherish lives to the last, pouring our energies into the relief of human suffering in more imaginative ways than killing the humans who are suffering.

Notes

1. *British Medical Journal*, October 2008.
2. http://www.dignityindying.org.uk/assisted-dying/assisted-dying-safeguards.html
3. Ibid.
4. Oregon Health Department report, 1998.
5. Oregon Health Department report 2004.
6. The organization was at that time called Compassion in Dying.
7. As Compassion and Choices was called at that time.
8. House of Lords Paper 86-II (Session 2004–05), p. 310.
9. Margaret Battin and others, Journal of Medical Ethics, 2007.
10. Ibid.
11. Barbara Glidewell, Oregon Health and Science University, Portland.
12. Dr Elizabeth Goy, Dept. of Psychiatry, OHSU. House of Lords Paper 86-I (Session 2004–05), para. 163.
13. Oregon Health Deparment report, 2000.
14. http://www.oregon.gov/DHS/ph/cdsummary/1999/ohd4806.pdf
15. Assisted Dying for the Terminally Ill Bill Committee, First Report, House of Lords, 3 March 2005.
16. Ibid.
17. Ibid.
18. *Daily Mail*, 9 December 09.
19. Assisted Dying for the Terminally Ill Bill Committee, First Report.
20. Ibid.
21. Ibid.
22. Ibid.
23. *Daily Telegraph*, 2 April 2009.
24. Ibid.

CHAPTER 3

EUTHANASIA IN LAW

A favourite morality tale of those who supported Lord Joffe's three failed parliamentary bills to have assisted suicide introduced to the UK legislature, between 2003 and 2006, was the so-called "Policeman's Dilemma". This featured a police officer who arrives at a road-traffic accident to find a fuel-tanker driver trapped in his vehicle and the lorry already alight. There is no chance of freeing the driver before the flames engulf him. He begs the police officer (who happens to be armed – this is probably America) to shoot him dead to spare him the agony of burning to death. Faced with apparently no alternative, the policeman obliges. Did he do the right thing?

The question is asked rhetorically, because supporters of euthanasia claim there is no moral alternative. And it follows that the same principle must be applied to the terminally ill; *in extremis* and in terrible pain, they are begging for the same release as the lorry driver. And if we accept the compassionate decision of the police officer, then we should rationally accept that the compassionate imperative is to dispatch the terminally ill on their request to do so.

There are variations to the Policeman's Dilemma. One such is another apocryphal story (though it is often claimed to be true) of a soldier whose phosphorus tank for his flame-thrower explodes, covering him in skin-immolating phosphorus. Again, he begs for his companion to shoot him. Do we condemn that comrade for doing so? Of course not.

The moral relativism of these fables can, of course, be challenged. The idea that there can be a subjective or objective universal morality attached to these actions, the breach of which can be justified by an overriding compassion, is to ignore that these can be instances that actually underscore the moral imperative to preserve life. They are, if you like, exceptions that prove the rule; the difference between sin and guilt. The supporter of assisted suicide might claim that this view is consistent with their justification for assisted suicide, the assistance to death being the compassion that overrides the formal immorality of the action. In reality, that is so; the doctor who increases opiate dosage, as the only practical option to relieve the unbearable pain of his or her patient, to levels that are potentially fatal to that patient should be held no more morally accountable than the poor policeman at the oil-tanker's cab (though, crucially, both will be subject to inquiry and professional accountability for their actions). As one witness to the Joffe parliamentary inquiry put it, he would indeed have pulled the trigger, but he didn't expect legally to be entitled to do so. In other words, we don't legislate for the shooting of lorry drivers who ask to be shot. We legislate against the shooting of anyone and then consider the circumstances, either in court or out of court (it may or may not be in the public interest to prosecute). Similarly, we legislate against assisted suicide in the Suicide Act 1961 and then treat cases on their individual merits.

Once, in law, we start to shift the burden of guilt away from the moral absolute that we call sin (if we are talking of separation from God's will), or that we call crime (if we are talking of the secular legislature), then we are morally compromised. And, in being so morally compromised, we may no longer be able to see that it was far preferable morally for the police officer never to have been put in the circumstance in the first place, either through improved road safety conditions or a more responsible fossil-fuels industry, and for the soldiers never to have been at war with phosphorus flame-throwers – and for doctors never to be in a place of moral dilemma, choosing between a patient's living hell and a lethal drug dose. The danger of losing that absolutist moral perspective is that we become recalcitrant in our aspirations. It becomes easier to concentrate our efforts on assisted-suicide clinics and lethal doses than it does on palliative medicine and end-of-life *living* care.

The circumstances in which we compromise an absolute morality with such relativism are precisely transferable from these hypothetical cases to recent actual legislative manoeuvres over assisted suicide in Britain. In the summer of 2009, just before the parliamentary recess in which they were to be abolished in favour of a new, attenuated Supreme Court, the Law Lords directed the Director of Public Prosecutions to clarify the circumstances in which a person would be prosecuted for assisting a suicide, in response to Debbie Purdy's appeal and the broader issue of some 115-plus assisted suicides by Britons at Dignitas in Switzerland not having been prosecuted. The non-prosecution "checklist" that the DPP subsequently introduced was precisely the kind of moral relativism that undermined the original intent of the law.

Assisting a suicide was and remains a very serious offence. In attempting to meet the remit placed upon him by the Law Lords, the DPP took what he intended and, indeed, appeared to be a neutral position between opposing views on the subject. In doing so, he shifted the moral ground on which the law is founded. As Peter Saunders, director of the anti-euthanasia group Care Not Killing Alliance, observed:

> His role... is to enforce section 2 (1) of the Suicide Act
> 1961 and, in this case, to set out the circumstances under
> which, exceptionally, he might decide not to proceed
> to a prosecution. The interim guidelines do not convey
> that message. They place the DPP in the position of
> an arbitrator between competing cases for and against
> prosecution rather than in that of an enforcer of the
> criminal law who may feel it appropriate, in specific
> circumstances, not to prosecute. To put it another way,
> the interim guidelines shift the centre of gravity of the
> DPP's position.[1]

So what the DPP had done is not only to step outside his brief, but also to produce draft "guidelines", subsequently amended and published as formal guidelines, which effectively undermine existing law on assisted suicide – law which, incidentally, is historically founded on a Christian premise of the quality of human life and death. We will look at those DPP guidelines in more detail in a moment. But first we should take a step back to examine the heritage of the law that the Law Lords and the DPP have so effectively derogated.

Law: Ancient and modern

It quite regularly serves the purpose of those who lobby for the legalization of assisted suicide in Britain to characterize the debate as being between compassionate, secular and post-modern reformers and medievalist religious fundamentalists who persist in considering suicide to be "sinful". To the extent that an ultra-conservative evangelical Christian, steeped in inerrant scriptural authority, may find plenty in the Bible to forbid suicide, the pro-euthanasia lobby can make progress with this argument and it has certainly been its parliamentary strategy on occasion to portray their apparently brave and humane campaign as being up against twenty-six bigoted bishops in the House of Lords and their supposedly brainwashed disciples. The scriptural case against suicide is founded on such passages as Deuteronomy 30:19:

> I call heaven and earth to witness against you today that
> I have set before you life and death, blessings and curses.
> Choose life so that you and your descendants may live.

Suicide was a major issue for Augustine in the fourth century. One of his better-known discourses noted that Christian women were committing suicide rather than being raped. For Augustine (bear in mind the patriarchal society in which he lived), women were not required to take their own lives to preserve their purity, because purity is a state of mind before God and physical violence could not despoil it. In this context he noted that Job retained his moral integrity despite his extreme physical suffering and resisted the temptation to take his own life. Augustine maintained that at no point does the Bible condone or make lawful the act of suicide. For Augustine, the sixth commandment, "Thou shalt not kill", applied as much to killing oneself as to murdering another. Or, rather, to take your own life is to commit auto-murder. The seventeenth-century Westminster Shorter Catechism, a key Calvinist text, tips its hat to Augustine in relating one of the Ten Commandments specifically to suicide: "The sixth commandment forbiddeth the taking away of our own life, or the life of our neighbour unjustly, or whatsoever tendeth thereunto." Samson's suicide, for Augustine, was an exception that proved the rule, since he was given a special divine dispensation. Augustine concluded: "He who knows it is unlawful to kill himself may nevertheless do so if he is ordered by God."[2]

Augustine exercised a powerful influence over Thomas Aquinas, who formalized a Christian theology against suicide, in a treatise of three arguments:

- Suicide is contrary to our nature, since every living creature desires or has a natural instinct for the preservation of its own life.

- Suicide abrogates our social responsibilities, as the whole human community is damaged by the loss of human life (a view that John Donne notably developed, as we shall see).

- Suicide contravenes our religious responsibilities, as God alone should decide when a person will live or die.

According to Aquinas: "To bring death upon oneself in order to escape the other afflictions of this life is to adopt a greater evil in order to avoid a lesser... Suicide is the most fatal of sins because it cannot be repented of."[3] In passing, we should note here a recurrent theme in the Christian attitude to suicide: that we "choose life" because, whatever it throws at us, it offers choices, whereas after death there is no such choice. This is significant in that it offers an antithesis to the consumerist viewpoint explored in Chapter 1, which offers that death should be a choice like any other. In actuality, it is entirely different from any other choices in life, because it shuts down choice in life permanently. William E. Phipps notes that Dante, following Aquinas' theology, placed those who take their own lives on the seventh level of hell, below the greedy and the murderous (*Inferno* 13).[4] For centuries those who committed the unconfessed and therefore unforgivable sin of suicide were not buried in cemeteries consecrated by Catholic priests. In tenth-century England, suicides were excluded from consecrated cemeteries and were buried at crossroads, with pagan practices such as driving a stake through the heart of the cadaver, a practice that can be traced as continuing until the 1820s.

The Jacobean metaphysical poet and Dean of St Paul's, John Donne, echoed Aquinas' second rubric on suicide in his piece of meditative prose, adapted to poetry:

> Any man's death diminishes me, because I am involved in
> mankind; therefore send not to know for whom the bell
> tolls; it tolls for thee...[5]

From Aquinas to the modern era, suicide remained a thoroughly un-Christian act. Phipps shows that Dietrich Bonhoeffer was indebted to Augustine when he wrote:

> God has reserved to himself the right to determine the
> end of life, because he alone knows the goal to which it is
> his will to lead it.[6]

Prior to his imprisonment and execution, a circumstance in which suicide would have appeared an admirable option, Bonhoeffer wrote:

> Even if a person's earthly life has become a torment for

him, he must commit it intact to God's hand, from which
it came.[7]

The Catechism of the Catholic Church, published in full form by Pope
John Paul II in 1994, begins its section on suicide with a preamble that
affirms that human life is not owned freehold:

> Everyone is responsible for his life before God who has
> given it to him. It is God who remains the sovereign
> Master of life. We are obliged to accept life gratefully
> and preserve it for his honour and the salvation of our
> souls. We are stewards, not owners, of the life God has
> entrusted to us. It is not ours to dispose of.[8]

The Catechism then re-affirms the tridentine ruling of Aquinas:

> Suicide contradicts the natural inclination of the human
> being to preserve and perpetuate his life. It is gravely
> contrary to the just love of self. It likewise offends love of
> neighbour because it unjustly breaks the ties of solidarity
> with family, nation, and other human societies to which
> we continue to have obligations. Suicide is contrary to
> love for the living God.[9]

The Catechism then takes off in a couple of intriguing directions.
The first has a very direct, if unintended, bearing on assisted suicide,
invoking the dangers of self-extermination to subsequent generations:

> If suicide is committed with the intention of setting an
> example, especially to the young, it also takes on the
> gravity of scandal. Voluntary co-operation in suicide is
> contrary to the moral law.[10]

"Scandal", in this context, is to be understood as "an attitude or behaviour which leads another to do evil". The second direction that the Catechism now takes is to view the suicide with far greater compassion than would have been tolerated by pre-Enlightenment ecclesiology:

> Grave psychological disturbances, anguish, or grave
> fear of hardship, suffering, or torture can diminish the
> responsibility of the one committing suicide... We should
> not despair of the eternal salvation of persons who have
> taken their own lives. By ways known to him alone, God
> can provide the opportunity for salutary repentance.
> The Church prays for persons who have taken their own
> lives.[11]

The softening of attitude to suicide resonated with change in the secular law in 1961. Hard as it might be to countenance now, to commit suicide prior to the Suicide Act 1961 was an offence and those who attempted suicide and failed could be prosecuted and imprisoned. Even the families of those who succeeded in killing themselves potentially could be prosecuted. This is law that can be seen to have grown out of Christian patristics, the doctrinal injunctions originally laid down by Augustine and Aquinas that self-murder is an offence against creation and consequently against God. But if even the orthodox Roman Catholic Church can reach a place where "we should not despair of the eternal salvation of persons who have taken their own lives", then clearly the judgments of those ancients are too harsh in the context of a developing world, in which theology is revised in the light of human experience. So suicide was decriminalized in 1961.

But the Suicide Act did contain an important clause, which has come to look like an anomaly to many, which ruled that those who assisted a suicide could still be subject to prosecution. Section 2(1) states:

> A person who aids, abets, counsels or procures the
> suicide of another, or attempt by another to commit

suicide shall be liable on conviction on indictment to
imprisonment for a term not exceeding fourteen years.[12]

This clause created a new offence of complicity in suicide. And its
consequence is apparently absurd; there is nothing like it elsewhere in
the law on causing death or injury to another person, because there is
no other instance in which an accessory can incur a liability where the
principal has not committed a criminal offence. In short, it became a
crime to assist with something that was not itself still a crime.

Supporters of the legalization of assisted suicide in Britain will
often point to this apparent anomaly. For the legislature to approve
suicide but to condemn the assistance of it, they argue, is to place
people at the most testing moments of decision over life and death in
the most intolerably vulnerable situation. It was the question of Debbie
Purdy's human right to clarity over how she could end her life and
what the consequences of actions to do so would be for her partner
that led the Law Lords in 2009 to instruct the DPP to state under what
circumstances those who assist in a suicide would and would not be
prosecuted.

The effect of that legal action, as we have seen, has been for the
DPP to shift the application of the law from enforcement of the Suicide
Act to the undermining of its provisions by arbitrating over when it will
have proved to be "legal" (that is, not subject to prosecution) to have
assisted a suicide. That represents not only a shift in the DPP's role, but
a very practical shift in the role of the Suicide Act. One of the effects of
section 2(1) of the Act is to protect the vulnerable, the terminally ill, the
frail and elderly from manipulation, exploitation or coercion by friends,
professional carers or family to end their lives. The motive could be
provided by the prospect of inheritance, or the desire provided by fear
of becoming a burden, on family or on society. The effect of the Suicide
Act has always been – and remains – a powerful disincentivisation for
those who would encourage the death of another.

That principle has been seriously undermined by what amounts
to a ginger group of suicide-sympathetic Law Lords directing the

DPP, off the back of the Debbie Purdy appeal, to "clarify" in law what factors are likely to influence prosecution of assisted suicide under the Suicide Act. In February 2010, the DPP published his guidance. Dignity in Dying and other pro-euthanasia groups put a brave face on it, but DPP Keir Starmer QC had backed off from commitment to many of their aspirations, leading to speculation as to the efficacy of this entire review initiative. Furthermore, as Prime Minister Gordon Brown pointed out in an article in the *Daily Telegraph*, publication of the DPP's clarification of the Suicide Act meant that the case for a change in the law to liberalize assisted suicide was now weaker or non-existent. He wrote:

> Following this clarification, and because of some
> important developments in care over recent decades,
> the case for a change in the law is now weaker... The law
> – together with the values and standards of our caring
> professions – supports good care, including palliative
> care for the most difficult of conditions; and also protects
> the most vulnerable in our society. For let us be clear:
> death as an option and an entitlement, via whatever
> bureaucratic processes a change in the law might devise,
> would fundamentally change the way we think about
> mortality.[13]

The law was now clear. And the only place it could be changed was in the parliamentary legislature, rather than through any back-door attempts at changing the law through the DPP's office.

The objective of the DPP's guidelines serving as an incremental step towards legalized assisted suicide in the UK had dissolved. From the DPP's draft guidelines, published in 2009, the list of public-interest factors in favour of prosecution doubled from eight to sixteen and there was one fewer factor against prosecution, at six (and a very important omission it was, which I'll come to in a moment). Doctors and medical staff were mightily relieved that he included their professions (including all nurses and healthcare professionals) as more likely to be prosecuted if they assisted a death, meaning that there was no creeping expectation of medics being required to dispense lethal doses. A new inclusion for prosecution was a "suspect... acting in his or her capacity as a person involved in the management or as an employee... of an organisation or group, the purpose of which is to provide a physical environment... in which to allow another to commit suicide." So the DPP was offering absolutely no prospect of sordid Dignitas-style clinics in Britain. And gone was the rather naive draft proposal for mitigation if "the suspect was the spouse, partner or close relative or a close personal friend of the victim", as if those close to the victim (and note the use of that word, incidentally) were less likely to have malicious intent in encouraging an assisted suicide. So bumping off granny when she becomes a burden, or for her money, is at least no closer as a prospect.

But by far the most important difference between the draft proposals and the final guidelines was the withdrawal of potential non-prosecution if (according to 2009's draft) "the victim had a terminal illness or a severe and incurable physical disability or a severe degenerative physical condition from which there was no possibility of recovery." Not only was this a triumph for the vast majority of terminally ill and disabled people who don't want to kill themselves and who certainly don't, thank you very much, want to be devalued as second-class lives by the euthanasia lobby. It also slaps down Dignity in Dying's much-vaunted mission statement on its website to provide "assisted death for terminally ill, mentally competent adults". The DPP has now stated unequivocally that being terminally ill makes no difference to prospects of prosecution.

This was a blow to the campaign of Lord Falconer and Dignity in Dying. But the expectation is that they will be back, just as soon as there's a prosecution under the DPP's new guidelines – and they make it more, not less, likely that people assisting a suicide will be prosecuted – Dignity in Dying will be claiming that the law must be changed in favour of voluntary euthanasia. Indeed, within weeks of the DPP's published guidelines, Dignity in Dying's chief executive, Sarah

Wootton, was writing to all MPs in a deft, watch-the-lady attempt to canvass sufficient support to claim that "most", or perhaps "a significant proportion", of the House of Commons supports a change in the law on assisted suicide, albeit meaninglessly in the context of a parliament that was about to face wholesale renewal within a couple of months at a general election. But this is a letter aimed at eliciting a helpful response from exhausted MPs at the fag-end of a Parliament, who probably don't have time or inclination to concentrate on the implications of what they are answering.

Ms Wootton's letter, after some ingratiating hand-wringing about how busy MPs are, read: "We believe terminally ill, mentally competent adults should, wherever possible, have control over where they die, how they die and, within strict legal limits, when they die." Not exactly the whole story there. Anyone would think Ms Wootton runs a palliative-care body. A much simpler and more accurate way of putting it, of course, is that Ms Wootton's organization campaigns for legalized assisted death and euthanasia.

She continued: "Our campaign is at the forefront of the social and political agenda and it is almost certainly an issue you will have to face at Westminster after the General Election." Really? The truth is that assisted suicide has failed consistently to get any traction in Parliament, has failed twice recently in the House of Lords and is even less likely to win time in the Commons, let alone be carried in a vote. And, even if it was on the parliamentary agenda, would the recipients of these letters really have had to face the issue after the election? Most of them seemed to be leaving politics or losing their seats.

But, of course, Ms Wootton had no real interest in researching MPs' actual voting intentions. She simply needed a knee-jerk response. Her sleight-of-hand questions were as follows:

(1) Most people will be able to have what they consider a dignified death if they have access to good quality end-of-life care. Do you support increased funding for good quality, patient centred care at end of life?

(2) The 2005 Mental Capacity Act gives statutory force to Advance Decisions (... Living Wills). Do you support the right of mentally competent adults, in advance, to refuse life sustaining medical treatment?

(3) Around 80 per cent of the public support a law which would give terminally ill, mentally competent adults the choice of an assisted death. Will you support a change in the law provided it includes strict safeguards?[14]

This was a hop and a skip through government funding for palliative care, to the right to decline treatment, to Ms Wootton's real intent: A medical profession that kills people. Happily, Dignity in Dying has little hope of changing the law, as the prime minister pointed out in his article on the subject, now that the DPP has clarified it on assisted suicide. But Ms Wootton's letter was a cynical attempt at manipulation nonetheless and a glimpse of the lobbying tactics yet to come on this issue. It will be an uphill struggle for that lobby – as we have seen, the law can only be changed in Parliament, not through the back door of the DPP's office when parliamentary efforts have dismally failed, as they have done under Lords Falconer and Joffe.

But it would be flippant to suggest that all attempts to change the law on assisted suicide are without merit. Supporters of legalized euthanasia in Britain regularly argue that the 115-plus people who have flown to Switzerland to end their lives, none of whom have caused those who have assisted them to be charged under the Suicide Act, would have been safer and more protected from any potential abuse had their suicides been under the legal regulation and safeguards of British law. They argue, not unreasonably, that to prosecute someone who has maliciously assisted a suicide after the event is of no earthly good to the deceased – far better to have protected that person with the kind of safeguards that Lord Falconer proposed in his amendments to the Coroners and Justice Bill in 2009 (two doctors' assessments and so on), while they were alive and through a system of legally scrutinized assisted suicide in the UK.

This is an evergreen argument that has been applied by those who want to liberalize activities in law, not always for motives that are directly attached to the protection of the vulnerable: Legalize proscribed recreational drugs, so that dealers are regulated and addicts are properly treated. Likewise, legalize prostitution, so that pimps and traffickers are made redundant and brothels can be regulated for hygiene and violence.

Applied to the debate over assisted suicide, such extreme legislative libertarianism has some appeal only so far as examination of its rationale. It advocates the introduction of something profoundly unattractive in exchange for strict regulation of its practice. Some will argue that social disapproval of some activities, reflected in law, only serves to force such activities underground, increasing the risks to those who are vulnerable to such activities. That is why the argument is applied to the markets for drugs and prostitution.

The business of assisted suicide and euthanasia is altogether different. For a start, there is no "market" for dying. Or there should not be – and the introduction of one, through euthanasia, should vigorously be resisted for that reason alone. We may regret it, but there are markets for prostitutes and drugs – there is demand, to which supply is provided. We can buy these goods and services, or choose not to. By contrast, death is a one-off event in life for everyone. There are, of course, accoutrements around our deaths for which a free market exist: Hospices, palliative care, life assurance and, ultimately, funerals and memorials are all subject to a supply-and-demand equation. But the buying and selling of death is a market from which we naturally retreat (though, as we saw in Chapter 2, countries which have adopted assisted suicide and euthanasia into their cultures have adopted such market techniques).

The proposal of assisted-suicide lobbyists in Britain is precisely and paradoxically that we should make it safe by introducing it. But there is an important distinction to be made in how the law works here. People are not driven to unsafe suicides abroad by the paucity of the British legal system; they choose to go abroad to take their own lives. That does not imply that nearly 120 assisted suicides abroad have made the British law an ass. Rather, it indicates three things: First, that these suicides have been treated with compassion in the British legal system, that the DPP is satisfied that there is a public interest neither in pursuing a case nor in prosecuting one. Second, there can be no such presumption of non-prosecution of those who assist them, should the 800-odd who are said to have expressed an interest in an assisted suicide abroad all execute their intentions; there must at least be a strong possibility that there are not a few within that tranche who have been dissuaded from assisting in a suicide that they know would not be viewed so compassionately under the Suicide Act. Third, the law in Britain reflects (or should) the kind of world we want to live in, the rule of law under which values of which we approve flourish. Just because our citizens go elsewhere to do something, unprosecuted, that is illegal does not mean that there are grounds for introducing the practice to the UK. If that were the case, we might have introduced child prostitution from south-east Asia.

And that is where the moral dimension cuts in on the management of our legislature. We make a distinction in law, as St Paul did, between sin and guilt, between our fallen nature and acts of wickedness. Similarly, we may consistently choose not to prosecute an act that is illegal, but it is important that we should be able to do so. Prosecution rates are not always the most effective assessment of a law's relevance. While it is important that justice should be seen to be done, it is yet morally consistent to enshrine in law actions of which we disapprove but rarely, if ever, prosecute (look at treason). Theologically, this is precisely the distinction between sin and guilt. If sin is a state of separation from the will of God, guilt is the state of being a sinner. While sin is an absolute and guilt is relative, a legislature founded on the principles of Christendom is going to abhor the former and accept the latter with a mixture of condemnation and compassion. All those who assist a suicide are going to be burdened with guilt, but dispassionate justice is nevertheless entitled to distinguish between the guilty and the criminally liable. In this distinction, we can abhor euthanasia and legislate against it, while choosing only to prosecute those cases in which we can establish that the guilt is criminal, rather than that which is likely to attach to any act that hastens the extinction of another human being.

Which brings us back to the Policeman's Dilemma. This fable caused some furrowed brows at the select committee hearing of 2005. Surely it should be simple – if the police officer acted with compassion in shooting dead the doomed lorry driver, then is it not logical to change the law accordingly? Not so, according to the Revd Canon Robin Gill of Kent University, one of four specialist "religious" witnesses before the committee:

> I would think what he did was right, but that is not the point. What we are here to argue is whether it would be right to change the law which allowed people to go round shooting people in accidents which clearly we do not do, at least I do not think we do. I hope the way the law would treat that person in that situation is in turn with real compassion. I think there is plenty of evidence to suggest that people who in desperation take the lives of dear ones, who are in intolerable situations, intolerable pain or distress, are treated leniently by the courts and I would hope that would happen. Clearly, a law which said… "In any future accidents, the police are entitled to shoot drivers at their discretion whenever they find them in a burning car"… I do not think that is how law could possibly work. What we are here arguing about is not about the taking of life: What we are arguing about is whether it is actually going to produce good benefits to society by changing the law on euthanasia. That is a very narrow question.[15]

It is, indeed, a very narrow question. And to those who ask why we have a law against assisted suicide, while apparently never prosecuting under it, there is a narrow answer: We don't allow the assistance of suicide any more than we allow the police to shoot drivers in burning lorries.

Notes

1. www.carenotkilling.co.uk
2. William E. Phipps, "Christian Perspectives on Suicide", *The Christian Century*, 30 October 1985, pp. 970–72. Copyright by the Christian Century Foundation; used by permission. Current articles and subscription information can be found at www.christiancentury.org. This material was prepared for Religion Online by Ted and Winnie Brock.
3. *Summa Theologica* 2-2, q. 64,5.
4. William E. Phipps, "Christian Perspectives on Suicide".
5. John Donne, *For Whom the Bell Tolls*.
6. William E. Phipps, "Christian Perspectives on Suicide".
7. *Ethics*, Macmillan, 1955, pp. 124–5.
8. *The Catechism of the Catholic Church*, Geoffrey Chapman (Cassell), 2004.
9. Ibid.
10. Ibid.
11. Ibid.
12. The Suicide Act, 1961.
13. *Daily Telegraph*, 24 February 2010.
14. Dignity in Dying letter to MPs, March 2010.
15. Assisted Dying for the Terminally Ill Bill Committee, First Report.

CHAPTER 4

THE MEDICAL FRONT LINE

In December 2009, a young doctor working in a hospital in Basingstoke, Dr Nicholas Ramscar, wrote to me, offering a piece on his experience of faith on the wards. Nick is an atheist himself, but evidently has a clear instinct for the value of treating the whole patient. His short article is entitled "Kindness on the Ward – An Atheist against Dawkins", and I reproduce it here because I think it demonstrates some of the intense complexities of the challenges of palliative care:

By any historical standards, I am enormously fortunate. Not just because, as Richard Dawkins has pointed out, existing at all is immensely unlikely, but because I am an adult male who has never had to face shellfire, poison gas, arrows or swords. Like Dawkins, my life so far has been unusual in its freedom from violence.

Despite my own good fortune, as a doctor I have witnessed the obscenity of a twenty-seven-year-old mother screaming from the pain in bones fractured by disseminated breast cancer, stood on wards in South Africa where four out of five were carrying HIV, and shuffled my feet awkwardly whilst talking to a surgeon of twenty years' experience who had been weeping the previous day. He had been trying to save the life of a child who had been swung head-first into a wall, by drilling holes in the skull to relieve pressure in the swelling brain. His efforts had failed.

These deaths, and all the quieter, commonplace ones from pneumonia and heart disease and strokes, are the result of damage to the genetic code or physical structure of the human body. Science alone can offer us any hope of progress against the BRCA gene that claimed that mother. Good public health and effective social services are what will save us from smoking-related diseases and violence against children. Appeals to loving energy, to crystals and chakras, are (as Dawkins makes abundantly clear) at the very best a childish distraction, which we really should have grown out of by now.

But let us return briefly to the room on the cancer ward where that young mother died. Outside, in the corridor where a few weeks later a man would die from a lung tumour that suddenly burst through the wall of an artery, her family were praying.

Religion is something that appears on the ward less often than I had anticipated, but when it does it is sometimes astonishing. I recently had to tell a man that his brain scan had shown that his headaches were caused by a tumour, probably a glioblastoma, which would undoubtedly kill him. He took the news so calmly that I thought he hadn't understood, whilst in fact he was a Christian who simply didn't see death as a big issue. Another favourite patient of mine with a throat cancer wished himself to death with an awesome lack of concern, again not seeing the end of this life as too dramatic an event.

It is too easy to point out that these people had chosen the religious meme most prevalent in their time and locality. They could hardly be said to be detached in their judgments, and of course the comforting effect of their religion is no argument at all for its objective truth. Dawkins has previously compared the calming effect of irrational beliefs to opiates, and I like to think that it was the morphine I administered that stopped that mother's screams, rather than the prayer on the other side of the door. But who are we, who have never seen a CT scan bearing our name and with a vile ball of genetic chaos nestling in the brain, and who have never felt the agony of infections overwhelming a crippled immune system that cannot fight back, to deny the power or legitimacy of an illogical comfort? Philip Larkin said, "Let us be kind to each other whilst there is still time" – we are all eventually under sentence of death, our cunning can only delay matters, and Dawkins is wrong to value cleverness over kindness.

I have quoted a favourite poet, and I would like to finish by considering a favourite quote of Dawkins'. Douglas Adams asked, "Is it not enough to see that a garden is beautiful, without having to believe that there are fairies living in it?" My question is: if you are lying alone in that garden, terrified and in constant pain, humiliated and betrayed by your body so that you can no longer control your own faeces and urine, is it so wrong to let go of harsh logic, and to hope that that body is not all you are?

*

I want to start my analysis of euthanasia and the medical profession with what might seem like a mawkish and sentimental story about a family pet. That is partly because I want to nail the argument that runs "We treat our dogs with more compassion than we do terminally ill people." But it also objectifies the killing process. I hope it shows, very simply, what it is. From that, we might glean more about what it is to be human and what makes that a very different condition.

A few years ago, we adopted an elderly golden retriever from a charity which finds homes for dogs whose owners have died or who can no longer cope with their pets. Very often, the charity told us, they were finding homes for much-loved dogs that would otherwise have to be put down. Scottie, as he was incongruously known, considering his breed, was a lovely old gent, with kind old eyes and floppy jowls set in a permanent smile as he panted with the exhaustion of his old age. We estimated that he must have been about fourteen years old. The vet found a large abscess under his thick, flaxen coat and cut it out, and Scottie perked up for a few months, though walks to the park were still punctuated with long stand-stills for him to gather his breath. We had him for about eighteen months, during which we often felt like his last nursing home, or even a canine hospice.

Then his condition suddenly deteriorated; he had an infected ulcer in his cheek, he couldn't seem to see or stand properly and, most distressingly, maggots had started to appear in the fur around his face. The vet, who had seen Scottie often, told us over the phone that nothing further could be done and his message was clear: We should decide when it was right to dispatch Scottie – and that moment should probably come soon. We found him in the garden and had to carry him to the car. At the surgery, the vet spread out a mat and explained that it was quite usual for there to be a little convulsion or whimper after she injected the massive dose that would stop his heart. But, in the event, Scottie died as he had lived, happily and gently. I found it far more moving than I had expected and wept copiously as we held his head and the vet held a stethoscope to his side to tell us when his big old heart had stopped beating. My wife said afterwards that it made her think of the whole euthanasia debate; neither of us was in the slightest doubt that we had done the right thing by Scottie and at the right time, but that he and we had enjoyed more than a year extra of his life that he wouldn't otherwise have had.

The argument is often made that we treat our dogs with greater compassion at the ends of their lives than we do fellow human beings in a comparable condition. It is said that, if the kindest thing to do to our pets is to end their lives when they are suffering and there is no hope of recovery, then the least we should do for our fellow human beings is to apply the same principle.

This view doesn't stand up to the barest scrutiny. Our animals, many of which have specifically been bred to be pets, do not have a human consciousness in the sense of understanding their own mortality or passage of life. As a consequence, animals neither rationalize their suffering nor enjoy rights as humans do; rather, we humans have responsibility for them, a responsibility that is entirely one-way, in that our pets bear no responsibility for us and our feelings. Put another way, it is utterly intolerable to keep a suffering animal alive because we cannot bear to be parted from it – unlike a dying sentient being who will understand a responsibility not to burden the living with the guilt of having caused their death. It should be added that our experience with a much-loved old dog isn't necessarily universal when it comes to the destruction of animals. As the charity from which he came told us, many abandoned dogs are simply put down. And not just abandoned ones; many that are simply inconvenient or no longer wanted are put down. The pejorative implications for a comparison with the case for euthanasia hardly need stating: But to spell it out, the idea that a transfer of the system we apply to dogs would lead only to compassionate euthanasia of humans is absurd. The logical extension is that we would simply be killing off those who had become a burden we couldn't afford, or who were simply soiling the furniture.

The analogy between destroying dogs and human euthanasia is worth developing not simply for the purpose of shooting down the justification of "compassion". It's also worth noting that the pro-euthanasia movement employs euphemisms such as "end-of-life care" and "helping to die" for an act that would directly be analogous with destroying a dog. Since some euthanasia supporters seek to make this comparison, it's worth following it through. We speak of "putting to sleep" when it comes to pets, but we also speak of them being "put down" or "destroyed". That is language that could as easily be applied to euthanasia, in place of those softer euphemisms. Consider the implications of having an elderly relative "put down" or someone with a terminal illness "destroyed". Put like that, it is little wonder that the medical profession wants nothing to do with the practice of euthanasia.

Morphine and medical myths

Having examined the legal position of euthanasia, it's time to direct our attention to what is and should be the nature of "end-of-life care" in the health service.

First, it's important to dispose of a couple of myths about "end-of-life" management by doctors. It is often said that doctors dispatch patients who are close to death and suffering with a massive and fatal overdose of morphine. Simon Jenkins, in *The Guardian*, even went so far as to suggest that "one-third of all registered deaths are caused by morphine overdose".[1] On the contrary, doctors who practise end-of-life medicine know the evidence that morphine, used correctly, is a very effective drug which can actually extend life by controlling pain and breathlessness and avoiding the exhaustion of unrelieved symptoms. Prescribing morphine properly is humane, compassionate and safe. It does not kill. Just because there is a last dose of a drug, it doesn't mean that it killed the patient dying of advanced disease. You might as well blame a final cup of tea, or the visit of a close relative, as a cause of death. To repeat, the prescription of opiates such as morphine can extend life at the last, by making the patient comfortable and the condition bearable.

The removal of life support is similarly described as a cause of death, as a premeditated act by medical staff. Again, this is to misunderstand the nature of end-of-life treatment. Doctors regularly discontinue futile treatment. But they don't do it in order to end a patient's life. They are simply recognizing that death cannot be prevented by treatment. We need to understand that end-of-life decisions, which are made every day by doctors, aren't the same as life-ending decisions. These are important distinctions, because such misapprehensions discourage some from entering hospital for treatment. In this regard, at least, it's perfectly safe to go into hospital.

The danger is that we should see the prospect of legalizing assisted suicide only in relation to the rights of the individual as enshrined in law. This tends to ignore the wider implications for our society and, in particular, how we wish to run our health service. The impact of a formal introduction of assisted suicide in Britain, as elsewhere, would be enormous, not least on clinical practice, because it would of course be doctors, nurses and health officials who would be required to provide the assistance with suicide, either directly or in its administration – an action often overlooked by euthanasia lobbyists, who might give the impression that assisted suicide is something performed entirely in private as an act between families and their "loved ones" (though, as we have seen, that kind of extended and unregulated system has developed in Holland). Killing someone is not easy, practically or morally, and it is glib and thoughtless to expect medical professionals to take it on.

So the potential effect of the introduction of assisted suicide on clinical practice is crucial to any debate on the subject. There is a widespread assumption that, if assisted suicide were legalized, it would simply become an accepted practice in the National Health Service. Bills presented to Parliament, such as Lord Joffe's three, have anticipated a system of assessment of suicide applicants and, not unlike in Oregon, prescription of lethal drugs by doctors. This presents one of the major tensions within the debate. The overwhelming majority of doctors in Britain are opposed to what is euphemistically called "assisted dying" and all the Medical Royal Colleges and the British Medical Association have, after consultation with their members, declared their opposition to it. Much has been made of the decision of the Royal College of Nursing, in July 2009, to change its policy towards assisting terminally ill people to commit suicide from one of opposing a change in the law to one of neutrality. In truth, the College's Council didn't think this was an important enough issue to call for a ballot of its membership. It saw fit to change the College's policy after a "consultation", in which just 1,200 or so members expressed their views, representing less than one third of one per cent of the College's 390,000 members. The RCN can be expected to return to the issue in a rather more democratic manner and there are those who expect this decision to be reversed. The role of nurses is critical to end-of-life care. According to Baroness Emerton, a former nurse:

> Patients will often unburden themselves to a nurse,
> in part because doctors are sometimes seen as being
> concerned solely with treatment. A good nurse can
> provide an effective channel of communication between
> doctor and patient, dealing with problems before they get
> out of hand and articulating them for the patient... On
> their shoulders rests a truly awesome responsibility – to
> help dying patients come to terms with their situation

so that, when the time comes, they can let go of life
peacefully and with dignity.[2]

So the role of nurses would be compromised forever by the introduction
of assisted suicide to the healthcare system. Baroness Emerton
continues:

> They would inevitably be involved at almost every stage
> of the process. Patients might well broach the subject
> with them and nurses could find themselves bearing
> some of the responsibility for assessment.[3]

Meanwhile, the medical profession continues to set its face against
assisted suicide. It suits the euthanasia lobby to suggest that opposition
to their proposals is led only by the religious. Lord Joffe has said that
opposition comes from people who are "under the influence of their
religious leaders". But most of the medical profession objects to assisted
suicide. The British Medical Association, the doctors' trade union, has
no truck with efforts to win over the medical profession to the idea of
killing their patients. In its response to the DPP's interim guidelines, it
wrote:

> Although the interim policy makes it absolutely clear that
> helping or encouraging another person to end his or her
> life remains a criminal offence, the BMA feels that some
> clarification of [this] factor would be helpful.[4]

That is nicely put. The BMA makes it abundantly clear that it wants
the Suicide Act 1961, which makes assisting a suicide punishable by up
to fourteen years in prison, to stay, while also making it clear that its
members want nothing to do with the practice. Surveys consistently
show that a majority of its members oppose any change in the law on
assisted suicide. And these are as likely to be clinical and professional
objections as they are to be faith-based objections (though some

obviously are informed by religious belief). Doctors are concerned about the dangers to the integrity of medical ethics and to the safety of their patients. They know how easily those who are ill can feel they are a burden and how ending life can become an easy option for the clinician. The fact is that opposition to assisted dying comes from a wide spectrum of opinion and profession, within Parliament and across society as a whole. And the medical profession has as wide a range of opposition to assisted suicide as any other interest group.

The General Medical Council stated its position most starkly in evidence to the 2005 select committee scrutiny of Lord Joffe's second assisted-suicide bill:

> A change in the law to allow physician-assisted suicide
> would have profound implications for the role and
> responsibilities of doctors and their relationships with
> patients. Acting with the primary intention to hasten
> a patient's death would be difficult to reconcile with
> the medical ethical principles of beneficence and non-
> maleficence.[5]

Pro-euthanasia campaigners maintain that, in those countries (examined in Chapter 2) where assisted suicide has been legalized, doctor–patient relationships have not been harmed. The claim is that patients continue to trust their doctors. But that really isn't surprising – patients have no alternative but to trust the doctors they have. According to the UK anti-euthanasia organization, Care Not Killing:

> The real point is that, when [assisted suicide] is
> legitimised as an integral part of health care, it acquires
> an aura of clinical respectability. We all of us assume, of
> necessity, that the advice we receive from our doctors
> and the treatments they administer to us will be those
> considered to be in our best interests, whether we feel
> they are or not. It is but a short step from there to the

notion that, if my doctor is prepared to prescribe a lethal overdose for me, he must regard that as an appropriate form of treatment for my medical condition and he must feel that taking my own life is preferable for me as a patient to dying naturally.[6]

So assisted suicide, claims Care Not Killing, is being placed within the comfort zone of a social service such as the healthcare system, which patients trust and which they assume, not unreasonably, is geared to protecting their interests. The pro-euthanasia lobby argues that a legalized system of assisted suicide would protect the interests of (properly assessed) patients who requested it because it would simply give them what they wanted. But this concept of a simple customer–supplier relationship is an extraordinary model to apply to the doctor–patient consultation. The professional practice of medicine is, or should be, a world away from the kind of market experience that we would associate with shopping for consumer items. The doctor–patient relationship is not about health-service supply meeting patient demand, however much the imposition of "internal" markets in the NHS has brought the vocabulary of commerce to medicine. A truly professional relationship requires the investment of trust by the patient in a doctor to provide impartial and very often unwelcome diagnostic advice and treatment, with the aim of restoring the patient to health, or to manage effectively the painful and otherwise distressing symptoms of an incurable illness. In the words of the GMC, it requires of itself "principles of beneficence and non-maleficence". That will include refusing to do things that the patient might want, such as prescribing antibiotics which aren't appropriate or which might, if prescribed, contribute to a degradation of antibiotic resistance in the community. Similarly, a doctor will decline to perform surgery which either carries unnecessary risk to the patient or is considered futile as a form of treatment. Legalizing assisted suicide within our healthcare system, simply on the basis that it is what the patient demands, would signal a dark and possibly irreversible development away from the beneficence principle, towards a simple commercial market in which it becomes the doctor's role to satisfy patient demand, however inappropriate that demand. And, as we have seen, the medical profession considers the request for suicide to be a deeply inappropriate one for doctors to meet.

The threat to palliative care

Legalized assisted suicide would also undermine the development of specialist palliative care, a branch of medicine in which Britain is a world leader. This is not so much because it would provide a justification for indolent or process-driven doctors, though there may be some truth in that. It is more that the overriding incentive to search for remedies to relieve intractable symptoms, in an environment where the preservation of tolerable life is the motive rather than the extinguishing of it, has led to some of the most significant breakthroughs in palliative medicine.

Baroness Finlay, who is Professor of Palliative Medicine at Cardiff University, recalls that when she qualified as a doctor in the early 1970s, palliative care was a primitive practice. It had only been a few years since Cicely Saunders, who is widely credited with having pioneered the post-war hospice movement with the foundation of the St Christopher's network, had opened the first hospice in the UK and begun her ground-breaking work to treat what she called "total pain" – suffering in body, mind and soul. By today's standards, there was little that could be done to remove physical pain and discomfort and to relieve the stresses and anxieties of terminal illness. Oddly enough, there was comparatively little pressure in this environment for the legalization of euthanasia or assisted suicide, though that goes some way to supporting the view that euthanasia is less the product of a more enlightened society than one of a society that has grown accustomed to the tyranny of "choice" and individualism in soft consumerism (see Chapter 1).

Finlay invites us to contrast the situation nearly forty years ago with today. "Palliative care has come of age," she says. It has been a recognized clinical specialism since the late 1980s, with lengthy and demanding training for those who wish to qualify. There are now specialist palliative care services in most major hospitals, in addition to voluntary sector hospices and community teams. According to Finlay, there are still "bad deaths", often because the distribution of specialist palliative care has not kept pace with the rapid advances that have been made in its quality, but they are rarer than they were. Concurrently, patients have realized that dying does not need to be synonymous with pain and overwhelming distress, and they no longer tolerate bad care. So the government has been under pressure to commit more resources to palliative and other end-of-life care to correct the deficiency.

The paradox which Finlay identifies is that the advances in palliative care have come at the same time as the increasingly strident demands for the legalization of assisted suicide. Given the improvements in palliative care, Finlay ascribes those demands to the growth of that post-modern individualism and its associated "lifestyle choices" which were discussed in Chapter One. Against this, doctors observe that, when someone feels hopeless and helpless as a consequence of illness (or, of course, depression), death may seem the only obvious solution to their problems. But, in an instance of medical science and pastoral religious ministry facing in exactly the same direction, they also note that often hope is restored by careful attention to the individual's values, restoring their sense of personal worth, and by helping them to find ways to achieve unfinished goals. This is the legacy of Cicely Saunders. This is far from the abstract ideals, the "motherhood and apple pie" values, that pro-euthanasia campaigners would claim are at the heart of resistance to assisted suicide. On the contrary, it's the pro-euthanasia lobby that assumes the existence of a perfect world, in which all doctors know their patients well enough to understand their underlying fears and anxieties and to assess whether a request for euthanasia stems from firm conviction or simply from a sense of hopelessness or obligation to relieve the burden of others. In the euthanasia enthusiast's perfect world, terminally ill people know their own minds clearly and always act rationally and understand perfectly the implications of the choice they are being offered, even *in extremis*. As Finlay confirms: "Anyone who works, day in and day out, among dying people knows that this idealised picture is simply not an accurate representation of what really happens."[7]

Finlay is better placed than most to know what really happens. She says that proposals for assisted suicide have "an air of unreality about them" that is worrying to anyone who has worked with terminally ill people. They assume that terminally ill people are entirely clear-headed and make life-or-death decisions on completely rational grounds. But the real world of clinical practice is not like that. "Many move during the course of terminal illness from hope to despair and back again," she says, continuing:

> Also important are the feelings of guilt that many terminally ill people feel at the burdens, real or imagined, that their illness may impose on their families. I am not talking about families callously pressuring terminally ill relatives to end their own lives but to hidden pressures that come from within the patient… Making assisted dying just another end of life "choice" may sound harmless enough, but one patient's choice can easily become another's risk. We don't have a choice about carrying personal firearms, because the end result would be more dangerous for us all. We must balance meeting the wishes of a resolute minority who say that they want to hasten their deaths against the risks of collateral harm to most patients, who want to live, but are vulnerable to wondering if ending their own life might be preferable to dying of their illness. I am in no doubt where that balance of harm lies.[8]

Finlay offers some personal insights into the dying experience:

I have come across instances in which an apparently firm resolve to die proves nothing of the sort. In 1991 a young man, a father of three children, was crystal clear in his repeated request to me for euthanasia. His clinical outlook was bleak. Against all predictions, he did not die. Eleven years later his wife died, leaving him to bring up their three children... In 2006 my own mother was in a hospice bed, in overwhelming pain, repeatedly saying that she wanted help to end her life. This was perhaps the greatest challenge to my view of assisted dying. But my mother was not "helped to die" (the current euphemism) by her doctors. Today, thanks to good hospice care, she lives independently at home despite her cancer and both her life and our lives are enriched.[9]

Her mother's subsequent death, in her own time in October 2009, will have done nothing to erode that enrichment.

Doctors who care for terminally ill people, explains Finlay, sometimes have the subject of assisted dying raised by patients. In most cases they want assurance that they won't be abandoned and will have care that maintains dignity and addresses their deepest fears. To respond by processing a request for assisted suicide risks sending a signal that the doctor agrees that the patient would be better off dead. We rely on our doctors to act at all times in our best interests. That inevitably gives them a degree of influence, however unintended, over the choices we make about our health.

Finlay argues that, in the real world, most people who receive a terminal prognosis are simply frightened individuals, whether it is fear of pain, of becoming immobilized, of incontinence, of loss of autonomy or dignity, or simply of the mystery of dying itself. Very few of them are able to say, calmly and without hesitation, that they accept their situation and want help to end their lives. The euthanasia lobby accepts this view and goes on to argue that, as a consequence, there would not actually be many cases of euthanasia if the law was changed to accommodate it. But, again, this assumption simply doesn't pass Finlay's "real-world test". In her words:

> It assumes that terminally ill people are either fully resolved that they want to end their lives or firmly opposed to such a course. In reality, the vast majority of people facing dying are ambivalent, oscillating between hopelessness and hope, worrying about being a personal or financial burden on those they love or that their own care costs will erode their descendants' inheritance. In a word, they are vulnerable, and it is a primary purpose of any law to protect the weak and vulnerable, rather than to give rights to the strong and determined at their expense.[10]

It is no coincidence that those countries which have legalized assisted suicide (we examined these in Chapter Two – Holland, Switzerland and the state of Oregon in the USA) have relatively poor records in the field of palliative care, or indeed have changed the meaning of palliative care once the administering of death has become clinical practice. In Britain, by contrast, palliative care has been a recognized clinical specialism, on a par with oncology or paediatrics, since 1987. We have, in addition to large numbers of inpatient and outpatient hospices, specialist palliative care departments in most of our major hospitals. One comment from Dr Bert Keizer, a Dutch doctor, in evidence to the House of Lords select committee, is worth quoting in this context. Accepting that euthanasia might possibly be justified "in certain exceptional situations", he nevertheless concluded:

> I would rather die in a country where euthanasia is forbidden but where doctors do know how to look after a dying patient in a humane manner than I would in a country where palliative medicine is ignored but euthanasia can be easily arranged.[11]

Pro-euthanasia campaigners rarely mention Holland these days. They prefer to cite Oregon as an example of palliative care improving following the legalization of assisted suicide in 1997. But while it is true that palliative care has improved there, it has improved in most countries in recent decades and, in any event, Oregon was starting from a relatively low baseline. The key point, however, is that the terms "palliative care" and "hospice" do not mean the same thing in Oregon as they do in Britain. Oregon does not have inpatient specialist palliative care beds or the intensive four-year palliative care training programme that we have in Britain. To many Oregon hospice doctors, palliative care is little more than a personal and part-time interest. It is largely limited to end-of-life care, whereas in Britain it is a specialism applicable to chronic as well as terminal illness. Comparisons between the two systems are not therefore meaningful and we cannot predict what might happen to specialist palliative care in British medicine under an assisted suicide regime simply by looking at what has happened to its less developed equivalent in Oregon.

No place for killing

Whether or not assistance with suicide should be legalized is largely a matter of personal and social values. But to legalize it as a therapeutic option within healthcare ("physician-assisted suicide" or PAS) carries with it the potential for damage to the ethics and standards of clinical practice and, therefore, ultimately to patients themselves. The pro-euthanasia lobby undoubtedly believes that the link with healthcare is important as a means of commending an otherwise unpalatable proposal to Parliament and the public. They also suggest that it would be unfeeling to require dying people to commit suicide without the support of their trusted doctors. It is hard to believe, however, that the few terminally ill people who are really serious about committing suicide would be deterred by having to use legalized procedures outside the healthcare system to obtain their prescription drugs. On the other hand, many more terminally ill people who are less resolute but who toy with the idea could well be encouraged to go through with taking their own lives by the comforting illusion that assisted suicide is a proper healthcare procedure. If we want to maintain the integrity of medicine and limit the practice of assisted suicide to the seriously determined and resolute, we need to ensure that it is kept separate from our healthcare system.

Doctors, in the most part, remain implacably opposed to any merger of the death industry with the healthcare system. Baroness Finlay, of course, considers that the case against medicalized euthanasia is overwhelming, but consolidates her opposition into two main reasons. The first is that it would have a corrosive effect on clinical thinking, by removing the pressure to redouble efforts to relieve suffering and restore hope; it makes ending life seem like a way out of a difficult situation for the doctor as well as the patient. And her other main reason is that this involves greater exposure of patients to danger.

Led by the General Medical Council, all the Medical Royal Colleges in Britain and the British Medical Association have, after extensive consultation with their members, declared their opposition to a change in the law to permit assisted suicide. These positions are hardly surprising. Doctors are, of course, trained to treat illness where they can and to relieve its symptoms where they cannot. This often involves decisions to cease interventions that are not achieving a benefit, doing all they can to improve quality of life and accepting that death is a natural conclusion to life. But the brief does not include deliberately ending a patient's life, even if that is what some of their patients say that they want. Respect for patient choice is a key ingredient of good clinical practice, but it can't override sound medicine. Choice does not mean that patients can have whatever they demand. If patient choice were the paramount consideration in clinical practice, then surgeons would be performing many unnecessary and harmful operations. The fact is that the relationship between a doctor and a patient is not the simple commercial one of a customer and a supplier, any more than buying an assisted suicide is the same as purchasing a car or a washing machine. As the GMC rightly observed, there is an ethical principle of beneficence. It is important that patients, who by their very circumstances are vulnerable, should be able to trust their doctors always to act in their best interests, even if those interests are not immediately apparent to an individual patient.

Advocates of euthanasia would like to present assisted suicide as potentially an integral part of the healthcare system. The strategy behind that is clear: It is widely – and rightly – assumed that a doctor will always act in his or her patient's best interests. It follows that a doctor's participation in assisted suicide confers on the act an aura of benevolence which commends it the more easily both to law-makers and to the public at large. Putting it outside the healthcare system exposes it for what it really is: killing people.

Those who want to see the law in Britain changed argue that there are compassionate grounds for embedding euthanasia in healthcare and that it would be hard-hearted to expect people who are suffering greatly and who want assistance to end their lives to be deprived of the support of their doctors in doing so. But, as with all law-making, the first priority must be to ensure that the interests of the majority are not prejudiced by any rights accorded to a minority. A vocal minority in the health system, in favour of assisted suicide, may well be jeopardizing the interests of a silent and vulnerable majority, who are not.

If someone is truly committed to ending their life, they will not be deterred simply because assisted suicide isn't part of the healthcare system. But doctors are being presented with the notion of assisted suicide within the comfort zone of healthcare, as just another therapeutic option, or something that those who fear being a burden on others simply ought to do. Even if they should decide against taking their own life, the problem does not go away. Some patients, while not opting for ending their lives, might feel themselves presented with a choice to be made at some stage in the future, a dark option that simply won't go away until at some point the patient gives in and decides on the suicide way out. It's like having the Grim Reaper standing behind the doctor on his ward rounds.

It has to be said here that state-sanctioned assisted suicide would inevitably introduce to the medical profession – and to society more broadly – the concept of a rank order in human life, that the lives of the disabled are of less worth than those of the fit and able-bodied, an attitude that has characterized some of the worst of contemporary totalitarian regimes. In response, the disabled can speak for themselves. And one of their most powerful voices comes from Baroness Campbell, who suffers from spinal muscular atrophy. Born in 1959, she was not expected to survive until her second birthday. She was scathing in her response to Lord Falconer's proposed (and defeated) amendment in 2009, delivering a speech to the House of Lords in which she said:

> By going with this amendment we turn the traffic lights
> from red to green on state-sanctioned assisted dying,
> albeit in another country... Those of us who know what
> it is to live with a terminal condition are fearful the
> tide has already turned against us. If I should ever seek
> death – and there have been times when my progressive
> condition challenges me – I want to guarantee that you
> are with me, supporting my continued life and its value...
> I tick every box of Lord Falconer's [criteria] to die. I could
> go tomorrow and, believe me, I would have no trouble
> in persuading two doctors. Three years ago two doctors
> persuaded me it was time for me to go on my way.[12]

Baroness Campbell claimed that assisted suicide is supported by only a small number of disabled people and that it represents an intention "to abandon hope and to ignore the majority of disabled and terminally ill people".[13] Movingly, Campbell was helped to sips of water during her speech and had to hand her text to a fellow peer, who read out the last part of it:

> If this amendment were to succeed I believe it will place a
> new and invidious pressure on disabled and terminally ill

people to think they are closer to the end of their lives.[14]

It must be conceded that Baroness Campbell's inspirational commitment to life, not to mention her breath-taking courage, is rare. She may set an example to which others aspire, but a valid argument can be constructed that she cannot deny others a different view of life and death than hers. The journalist John Diamond memorably wrote a book about his own terminal illness titled *C: Because Cowards Get Cancer Too*, which pithily rebuts the notion that everyone can, or especially should, be brave and forbearing about their final condition. But the answer, medically speaking rather than for spiritual or social reasons, is not to give the suicidal what they apparently want and not just, as Baroness Finlay confirms, because the moods of patients swing, sometimes over the long term, between despair and hope. The key point here is that, once the disabled are enabled to dispose of themselves, they become disposable.

Debbie Purdy, who campaigned for legal clarification in 2009 of the circumstances under which her partner would be prosecuted for helping her to die, in this regard unintentionally did great harm to the public perception of the multiple sclerosis from which she suffers. Multiple sclerosis is an awful disease and can be terminal. But it remains true that for most of those with MS, it is something they live with, rather than die from. An unintended consequence of Purdy's campaign is for public perception to shift towards MS being a death sentence, though most sufferers are living long and full lives. Little wonder that the Multiple Sclerosis Society wrote in its submission to the DPP's assisted-suicide consultation:

> Due to the inherent uncertainties experienced by people with MS, those who have been newly diagnosed often express fears about how the condition will affect their lives, leading some to consider the end of life.[15]

Again, this is about a life and medical challenge that an organization such as the Multiple Sclerosis Society helps people through, rather than referring them somewhere where they can access a lethal dose. As the MSS says in its recommendations to the DPP: "Address the fact that there is not a universal understanding of what constitutes a 'terminal illness.'" Not universal, not within the medical profession, nor even in the course of a single person's life.

Finally, it is worth mentioning that doctors and nurses in the palliative and end-of-life care practices speak of commonly held myths about the process of dying. They claim that most people believe that most deaths are painful and difficult, when most are not; that deaths invariably require the prescription of opiate drugs, when they do not; and that doctors accept these canards as fact. Perhaps the most widely held myth is that doctors routinely prescribe lethal doses of opiate, or leave the means of suicide "in a drawer by the bed", like a razor-blade in the condemned cell, a myth that the documentary maker Ray Gosling perpetuated in 2010, when he claimed to have suffocated a lover dying of AIDS, with a doctor's collusion, which led to a police inquiry. None of these myths bears scrutiny; the briefest conversation with a palliative-care doctor will reveal that the overwhelming majority of deaths are comfortable, if spiritually demanding for all who are close to them. Perhaps the most important point of all here is that the quality of death for the majority would be compromised permanently by allowing euthanasia in law for the tiny minority who demand it. This may be a utilitarian argument, but it doesn't lack potency.

In summary, it is a paradox that, as medicine has begun to cope effectively with the symptomatic problems of terminal illness, demands for a legalized form of euthanasia have become more strident. This paradox can be explained by recognizing that the motives for assisted suicide are driven by the growth in our society of a secular individualism and the increased emphasis on notions of autonomy and personal control that were discussed in Chapter One. Baroness Finlay demonstrates how recent proposals for legalization of assisted suicide in the UK fail the "real world" test of clinical practice and terminal suffering. Whether or not we can accept the principle of assisted suicide depends essentially on one's personal or social values, but it has to be said that the case against medicalized euthanasia is particularly strong. Euthanasia as part of the healthcare system – and therefore a therapeutic option – conflicts with good medical practice and introduces a quasi-commercial, customer–supplier relationship into doctor–patient relationships. And because it seeks to set assisted suicide within the comfort zone of healthcare, it disguises its real, defeatist nature and thereby exposes the vulnerable to greater risk.

Notes

1. The Guardian, 22 October 2008.
2. Baroness Emerton in an article entitled "A truly awesome responsibility" in *Nursing Standard*, quoted on Dying Well website, http://www.dyingwell.org.uk
3. Ibid.
4. BMA's submission to the Director of Public Prosecutions, 2009.
5. House of Lords Paper 86-I (Session 2004–05), para. 108.
6. Care not Killing website, www.carenotkilling.org.uk
7. Dying Well website, www.dyingwell.org.uk
8. *The Times*, 1 April 2009.
9. Baroness Finlay, *The Times*, 1 April 2009.
10. Dying Well website, www.dyingwell.org.uk
11. House of Lords Paper 86-III (Session 2005–06), p. 55.
12. Baroness Cambell of Surbiton, *Hansard*, 7 July 2009.
13. *The Guardian*, 7 July 2009.
14. Baroness Cambell of Surbiton, *Hansard*, 7 July 2009.
15. Submission from the Multiple Sclerosis Society to the Director of Public Prosecutions, December 2009.

CHAPTER 5

WHY SUFFER – FOR CHRIST'S SAKE?

A friend has written to tell me the story of Alison Davis, because he's heard I'm writing this book. In addition to spina bifida and hydrocephalus, and using a wheelchair full time, Alison also has emphysema, a breathing problem that makes her susceptible to chest infections, arthritis, lordosis and kyphoscoliosis – causing her spine to twist out of shape in every possible direction – and osteoporosis, or brittle bones, which has caused her spine to collapse and trap nerves. When the pain is at its worst, she "can't move or think or speak", as she puts it.

In the late 1980s, pain of various sorts compounded to make her feel she wanted to die. Over time, her desire to die became a settled wish and lasted about ten years. She attempted suicide several times. If euthanasia had been legal then, she says she would have requested it with no hesitation at all. "I would have satisfied all the supposedly 'strict criteria' which pro-euthanasia groups want, and which are mandatory in places where euthanasia or assisted suicide is legal. It took my friends, and particularly Colin, my full-time assistant, many years to persuade me that my life did have value."

Their efforts and a trip to India in 1995, during which she met disabled children, whom she later began to support financially, helped to turn her life around. After that trip she told Colin: "Do you know, I think I want to live." It was the first time she had thought that for over ten years. Had euthanasia or "assisted suicide" been legal, she says she would have missed the best years of her life.

She writes: "My life has been full of pain and suffering, true. But it has also been one long adventure, with great highs and great lows. I think my eventual death will also be an adventure – but for now I'm content to wait for that particular adventure to come naturally, in its own time."

When I read this, I replied to my friend that it was "a wonderful story of resurrection". I've dwelt on that thought since; how the stories of Alison Davis, or Charlotte Raven realizing that she was truly alive only when she visited those suffering from the same terminal disease as her, or Lady Campbell in her wheelchair in the House of Lords who was meant to have died before her second birthday, are resurrections in the midst of life, the triumph of life over death, of hope over despair, of love over abandonment.

*

I have looked at the inadequacies of euthanasia in medicine and in law. I hope I have looked at it culturally, socially and in the political context too. But where is God in this? A slick and true answer to that is that he is in the politics and the law in their affirmations of the value of human life and in the medical profession; in the context of the latter, the Christian is going to believe that God's work is particularly well served by those scientists who have made such advances in the preservation of precious lives and in palliative care for those lives at their end. Revelation of God can only be made in the context of the world in which we live and the lives we live in it, not as some separate, mystical experience that has no bearing on our human experience.

All that is valid. But it remains the case that many of those who would introduce euthanasia misrepresent the Christian faith on the issue. It suits them to do so. They will portray Christian opponents of euthanasia (and those of other faiths) as under orders from their "religious leaders", as if the household of faith is populated with mindless automatons. They will claim that we are "religious fanatics" with a desire to see people suffer, or to exercise some kind of spiritual control over them.

All that is untrue. Or, at least, it is untrue for the overwhelming majority of religious people in anti-euthanasia organizations, in the medical professions and in Parliament. Of course faith informs these people in the entirety of their lives, but also in the reality of their lives, in the context of what they witness, not as some separate ideology or adjunct, or a set of discrete values that are worn like layers of clothing.

Surprising as it may seem to those who have already made their minds up before meeting any, religious people have restless, inquiring and rational minds. They struggle to make sense of life and death. They reach different interpretations and conclusions. Some of them, indeed, conclude that euthanasia is compatible with God's plan for the world. And, in the most part, we respect each other, or try to. But on one thing most of us agree: There is not a narrow, simple set of rules to which we must adhere to be people of faith. For Christians, it's more a case of a developing, two-millennia adventure with God (and that's the adventure, I believe, to which Alison Davis refers), with much, much more to come.

But our tradition is richer in human thought and the struggle to understand the mind of God than our detractors would claim, for whatever motives. So it's incumbent on those whose faith informs them in their opposition to euthanasia to make a case for their theology. That warrants a book in its own right. But, here, I want to make a case for a developing theism that is incompatible with the destruction of human life, even when that life is subjected to suffering and close to its end, and I want to explore what the interpretative doctrines attached to the end of the life of Jesus Christ have to tell us about the business of assisting suicide. I relate this brief exposition of theology not in an evangelistic or, I hope, in a proselytising way; I am conscious that very many people don't and won't subscribe to this worldview. Indeed, many of the Christian faith too will diverge on what I have to say here. As for those who don't share this faith, or any other, I hardly expect it to persuade them from their own position. But it's better that we understand each other, "where we're coming from", in the common phrase, rather than making simplistic assumptions about where our opponents stand on the issues of a given life and a chosen death. And, perhaps most importantly, there are some pretty hideous misrepresentations of what Christians believe out there, so this quick excursion through the Christian understanding of human suffering is intended to demonstrate that we are neither mindless control freaks, nor under the cosh of some cruel archbishop. Christians have struggled with suffering for a couple of thousand years and their story is, at least, worth listening to.

Suffering: What's God got to do with it?

A mighty protective wall has surrounded classical conceptions of God for a couple of thousand years, before more liberal and open theisms laid siege to it in the twentieth century and through the post-modern era. The protective bastion for classicism was most durably built by the Greek school of philosophers, who hijacked the vulnerable and sometimes violent God of the Hebrew scriptures and encased him in a sarcophagus of immutability and perfection. It was this patristic view of God that endured through the traditions of Augustine and his alliterative medieval successors, Anselm and Aquinas and beyond, to the Reformation revival in classicism with John Calvin and even through to its contemporary apologists, such as Paul Helm, of whom more in a moment.

Plato is to blame, some four centuries before the birth of Christ, and the Middle and Neoplatonic schools that he spawned were to provide classicism's longevity – though Philo, writing coincidentally around the time of Jesus' ministry, must also take the rap. He tried to reconcile the Hebrew scriptures with Platonic thought, writing a treatise called *On the Unchangeableness of God* and playing his part in consigning God to the transcendent heavens of what theologians call immutability and impassibility. Being "impassible" meant that God was unable to suffer: this doctrine is vital to an understanding of God's engagement with human suffering.

According to classical theism, God is not only entirely separate from his creation, but his divine perfection means that he doesn't need it in any way at all. The classical argument runs that it is an act of the purest grace that he should have created something impure, but any dependence upon it (and therefore upon us) would compromise his perfect independence. In short, he is in charge, but unaffected. This is because any effect on the divine would involve change and, since God is perfect, any such change would have to be for the worse. As well as immutability and impassibility, God is "simple" in the sense that there can be no differentiation within the Godhead (or the Trinity) and no separate or spare parts; he is a "pure act", in that any change would imply incompleteness, and he is "timeless", in that the eternal Word has no before or after, only an eternal present.

As Augustine wrote: "Only what does not only not change but also cannot at all change falls most truly... under the category of being."[1] Importantly, classical theists hold that God has ordained everything, including all evil and human suffering for reasons beyond our comprehension, and that he is beyond any mortal understanding or influence. He cannot change his mind, so prayers have no effect upon him. You begin to see where the idea came from that humans had to suffer the terrible rigours of terminal illness until they were released by death, because it was all in God's perfect plan, for reasons we couldn't begin to understand but which we had to bear patiently because it was in our best interests to do so. This is a concept that was to drive the determinism of Calvin and his doctrine of unconditional election, over which we enjoy no independent will. Similarly, God has wholly complete knowledge of our future history. In the classical tradition, God owns and knows our future. Humans have free will only in so far as they act upon their desires, which anyway are determined by God. So, in what is called a "compatibilistic freedom", humans will behave always as God desires.

This is a fairly austere view of the human condition and our relationship with God, and may sound downright cruel to contemporary ears. It's unlikely to get much traction these days as a justification for physical suffering, even among most Christians, but bear with me; I'm not suggesting that we adopt a classical theistic approach to end-of-life care. Theology was to develop on these issues in the post-Enlightenment era. But it's important to know how we got there. It certainly seems extraordinary to the post-modern mind that anyone can hold to these intransigent absolutes, but Vancouver-based theologian Paul Helm has a go.[2] In respect of divine foreknowledge, Helm seeks refuge in the Augustinian–Calvinist tradition and argues from a broadly Augustinian position that it is reasonable to believe that divine foreknowledge of what's going to happen to us and human freedom are compatible. He further argues that Augustinian divine foreknowledge does full justice to divine omniscience and is simpler than rival doctrines.

It's important to make these points about classical theism and what it says about our understanding of God's will historically, because it shows what an alternative "open theism" was up against and how it changed our Christian understanding of suffering, when it started to prosper as a theology in the 1980s. People such as the open theist Gregory Boyd rejected, from human experience, the rigidity of classical theism and

> the Calvinist view that the work of the Holy Spirit is
> irresistible. People can and do resist the Holy Spirit and
> thwart the will of God... Hence we affirm that if a person
> is saved, it is all to the glory of God, whereas if a person is
> damned they only have themselves to blame.[3]

That human experience to which I refer was all to do with secular matters and human affairs, which gave open theism its genesis. The sheer scale of human suffering in the twentieth century, such as the "perverted science" of the Nazis, as Winston Churchill put it, for instance, and widespread awareness of it as a consequence of the growth in mass media, forced classical theism into retreat. The question of how a perfect God could be the creator of the unparalleled carnage of the First World War, the Holocaust of the Second, the atom bomb and the plight of the Third World became hollow and rhetorical. It was human actions, rather than philosophical theology, that challenged the hegemony of classical theism. And with it, of course, went the idea that we should suffer the agonies of terminal disease and old age, because they were given to us to bear by God for his own mysterious reasons.

Alternatively, according to open theism, in his act of creation God consented to open a wide, even infinite, range of future possibilities based on how the free creatures of God would react to a universal offer of unconditional love. The work of the German theologian Jurgen Moltmann can't go unremarked here (Moltmann is actually a "kenotic theist" – *kenosis* is the Greek term for God "emptying himself" of his divinity to experience humanity in Christ – but that distinction needn't delay us here). He gives us a construct in which the death and resurrection of Christ provide us with a model of how to deal with human suffering and in which, consequently, God has a loving solidarity with the world in its suffering. But more of that when we come to the doctrine of the atonement and its message for human suffering.

For now, all we need to note is that the motivation for the new, open-theistic view is that it arises from the notion that the triune God created humans with the ability not only to experience divine love, but to choose whether or not to reciprocate with human love. In other words, life is a team event, in which God joins in with human suffering – and that, of course, has a resonance with classical theism. Open theists share with classical theists the view that God is perfect, immutable and omniscient. But they suggest that suffering has a divine purpose: the dark places of life are where we get into the same trench with God. In this way, open theists believe that God experiences rich, reciprocal relations with his human creatures, in all areas of their lives and, indeed, deaths.

So evil is allowed but not desired by God and, while it can't be said that everything that happens is ordained by God, he has chosen to exercise "general providence" rather than "meticulous providence"; he wills the best for us in the building of his Kingdom, but his will can sometimes be thwarted. It follows that the future isn't under God's direction, because he has chosen not to create it, only its possibilities, and it therefore doesn't exist other than in divine and mortal aspirations. It's open theism precisely because, for both God and us, the future is open. The important development of thought here, conditioned by the traumatic events of the twentieth century, is that far from walking into a future prescribed by God (or, at least, the good and holy bits), as the classical theists would have it, we embark together into the adventure of the future, in which we have, by God's grace, been granted both the freedom to depart from God's plan and the path to rediscover and return to it. In this way, though we can perpetrate Hiroshima and the Holocaust, we continue to share Paul's sure and certain hope of being redeemed from such mortal horrors.

This argument, of course, presents us with a libertarian God. And one that suits our times. William Davis sardonically ascribes several post-modern reasons for open theism flourishing, very much in keeping with the individualism that characterizes our world and which we looked at in Chapter One: suspicion of authority; infatuation with liberty; impatience with mystery; pragmatism about community; and the emergence of "extra-ecclesial Christianity". He concludes dolefully that "open theism will thrive in this freedom-intoxicated, authority-distrusting age".[4]

This analysis goes some way to explaining why a Christian apologetic can be made for assisted suicide and/or euthanasia. If God hasn't pre-ordained how we are to live and, importantly, to die, then it is no part of a divine purpose to have someone (whom he loves unconditionally, remember) dying in prolonged pain from an incurable condition. He would surely long, with us, for that person's release from their suffering. So bring on the sacramental assisted suicide (which is a pithy paraphrase of Professor Paul Badham's book, with which I started this one). But we should also note the shift of emphasis that was a consequence of open theism, in the context of the suffering of the twentieth century, from the atonement of Christ to his resurrection. In the classical model, Christ's sacrifice of himself to suffering and death is one that is made by the second person of the Trinity in atonement for the sins of mankind – it is the price that God pays on behalf of mankind to level the balance sheet. And it is a sacrifice made in the place and on behalf of mankind. As a consequence of the twentieth-century experience of suffering and the emergence of open theism, the atonement is to a significant degree superseded by the Passion and resurrection of Christ. On that kenotic model, God empties himself of his divinity to share our suffering and redeem it in his defeat of death in the resurrection. So, in making sense of the suffering in God's creation, theology has moved away from the Lamb of God's sacrificial nature in the atonement towards a sense that the Christ story is a revelation of God's enthusiasm to share and bear our suffering and to redeem us through it.

We will come to a more detailed examination of the role of the atonement in the next section. Meanwhile, the unavoidable and radical conclusion of this examination of open theism is that, from a Christian perspective, it is a necessary part of human experience to encounter the divine in our shared physical suffering, as well as in life's high summer. This is emphatically not a charter for the holiness of agony, self-immolation and the waving away of palliative medicine. It is, however, a justification for going the extra mile in this life, or so far as we possibly can, in order fully to comprehend the divine–human partnership. And it is Christ-like to do so. We might, like him, in our Gethsemane moment, pray for this cup to pass from us (as Alison Davis repeatedly did). We might even sweat blood, one hopes only metaphorically, at the prospect of what awaits us. The joint venture to which we're conscripted provides a fresh dynamic to the utterance, "Thy will be done" – not a slavish obedience, but rather an embarkation on a mutually reliant enterprise to its whole completion.

Jurgen Moltmann, whom I want to consider in a moment in respect of atonement doctrine, finds a way of reinterpreting a God who shares, rather than simply witnesses, human suffering, when he writes that "there would be no 'theology after Auschwitz'... had there been no 'theology in Auschwitz'":

> A God who cannot suffer is poorer than any man. For a
> God who is incapable of suffering is a being who cannot
> be involved. Suffering and injustice do not affect him.
> And because he is so completely insensitive, he cannot be
> affected or shaken by anything. He cannot weep, for he
> has no tears. But the one who cannot suffer cannot love
> either. He is a loveless being.[5]

For our purposes, that is a hugely relevant passage, and not just because it underscores the depth of interdependence in the joint venture of humanity and God (if you replace the word "God" in the passage with "person", it remains utterly valid). But, in addition, it demonstrates what has occurred in the Passion of Christ in relation to our own mortal suffering. The Passion is associated with our suffering, not so much as an act of atonement as an act of love. According to the comparative theologian Keith Ward, "God shares in the pain and permits the wayward freedom of creatures in order that, finally, creatures should share in the bliss and become vehicles of the truly creative freedom of the divine nature."

In further struggling to understand the purpose of suffering in God's creation, we need to broach another school of thought – process theology, in which the world is interpreted as being entirely contained within God (though not as in pantheism and Hinduism; in process theology God includes everything, but everything isn't God). The project of life is work in progress, a process and a journey through time to a destination known to God, with "occasions of experience", as the founder of process theology, Alfred North Whitehead, called the basic building-blocks of our reality. So process theology represents, among much else, a practical and contemporary interpretation of the purposes of risks and suffering in human experience:

> Should we risk suffering, in order to have a shot at intense
> enjoyment? Or should we sacrifice intensity, in order to
> minimise possible grief? The divine reality, who not only

enjoys all enjoyments, but suffers all sufferings, is an
Adventurer, choosing the former mode, risking discord
in the quest for the various types of perfection that are
possible.[6]

It is here, perhaps more than elsewhere in theism, that process theology
delivers us a partner-God, with whom we share life's journey, with all its
joys and horrors, in whatever proportions, because the destination is
one that we can only reach together. It follows that each of our journeys
needs to be continued to an absolute conclusion in order for them to
make the most sense, rather than a conclusion of our own convenience.
Otherwise, we would not only bail out of this life when the going gets
intolerably tough, but we might as well do so when the aches and pains
and lack of potency of late middle age cut in. This is not to imply that
there is a "perfect" lifespan – the baby who dies, the car-crash victim,
the young casualty of war all have lives that are complete in Christ.
We don't know how, but that's "the sure and certain hope of the
resurrection". But to opt for self-destruction to avoid an experience that
we fear may be also gratuitously to refuse an opportunity for further
enrichment and, consequently, revelation. Every life can be redeemed
(even, especially, the suicide), but that is no incentive to throw away,
avoid or opt out of the experience. And not just for the one who lives
the life, but for those who are loving witnesses to it too.

Yet how can we understand this partner-God, who offers to
accompany us on a dangerous journey until, as it were, our "luck" runs
out, who still owns the attributes of omniscience and omnipresence of
the classical theistic school, while emptying himself of his divinity to
join us at our level of human suffering? It's important to answer this
question, because it is likely to be the same answer for the question,
"What have I got to live for?" And if we don't have an answer to that
question, then we have no case to offer in theology against an assisted
suicide or euthanasia.

We need concede nothing of the universality and unconditionality
of God's love for his creation in a post-modern conception of him (or

her, for that matter, as we shall see in a moment). But a resolution is required, if we are to construct an interpretive model of God that takes account of the bridging of a transcendent, distant and disengaged creator of the classical school with an intimately involved participant in his own creation, without one trumping or diminishing the other. Our divine partner in the rigours of living can only make sense, can only be seen to shoulder our burden, if we see him through attributes that we understand. It's not helpful for everybody and perhaps too glib to say that the answer is Jesus. We need new metaphors through which to understand our partnership with divinity.

That's a search in which we should not be afraid. It's not searching that we should fear. The patient dying of a terminal disease may well reject the old, patriarchal and despotic images of deity offered by a classical theism and, as a consequence, the partnership offered by an open or process theism breaks down on the human side. This is a problem for any priest or anyone else ministering in a hospice or elsewhere with the dying. The metaphorical theologian Sallie McFague writes:

> religious language is a problem for us, a problem of a
> somewhat different kind than the classical one. For most
> of us, it is not a question of being sure of God while being
> unsure of our language about God. Rather, we are unsure
> both at the experiential and the expressive levels.[7]

McFague offers us metaphorical representations of God that embrace the scientific, the socio-political and the social, straying well away from the traditional strictures of "God the Father". We might agree with Simone Weil, when she says, "I am quite sure that there is no God in the sense that I am sure there is nothing which resembles what I can conceive when I say that word." But we can be sure that a conception of a God that is manageable would be infinitely helpful for someone needing to understand the divine partnership at the end of their life and wondering why they might have more to gain from that partnership by placing that life unconditionally in the hands of their creator, than by taking it by their own hand.

Death on the cross road

If the transition of our view of the nature of God from a classical theism to a God, viewed through the prism of open and process theisms, goes some way to explaining that God joins us in our human experience, it doesn't necessarily tell us how he does it. That's where the Christian narrative of the atonement arises. It's at the cross that human suffering meets God, by which I mean that it is through the suffering of the Christ at his crucifixion that we begin to glimpse a divine purpose to our suffering and the way in which God has chosen not just to experience our suffering in the incarnation, but to meet us in it. It is the supreme Christian enactment of redemption through suffering, and we should examine briefly what it has to say about the revelation of divine purpose at the ends of our lives. Calvary is where every bloody sinew of our humanity strains upwards to the heavens, while the walls of divine perfection are breached to enable God to join us in human death. And where, paradoxically, God is never closer than when we seem furthest apart, in those moments where we ask, with the Christ, "My God, my God, why have you forsaken me?" It is worth just briefly outlining the various doctrines of Christ's atonement.

The Bible accounts of the death of Jesus offer us five interpretations of the atonement: Christ as victor over Satan (or evil); Christ as reconciliation; as propitiation; as a sacrifice and as the obedient servant. In this last category, Christ submits himself entirely to the will of God in his servant ministry. The washing of his disciples' feet at the Last Supper and the submission in the Garden of Gethsemane are potent signifiers of this role. Christ recognizes his Messiahship in the prophecies of Isaiah about the suffering servant of God. John's Gospel emphasizes this aspect of Christ's purpose and Paul offers his apostolic weight to it, arguing that we are justified – that is, reconciled to God – through Christ's obedience. And we learn of this obedience through the pain and suffering of the Passion (Paul wrote: "He humbled himself and became obedient to the point of death – even death on a cross", Philippians 2:8).

Whether the Christ is viewed, in biblical terms, as an obedient servant or a sacrifice for a wrathful God, which is the model that is called the doctrine of "satisfaction", his suffering is seen to have had a divine purpose. Indeed, the divinity is within the suffering itself; this is the difference between the ancient doctrines of *hoc significat* (the Passion representing God's suffering) and *hoc est* (it actually being God's suffering). The purpose of the suffering of the atonement has its climax and most expressive fulfilment in Jesus' final cry from the cross in John's Gospel: "It is finished." Translation from the original language is never perfect, but the phrase carries less of the weight of an ending than of a sense of Christ's mission being complete, seen through to the end, the work of God having been accomplished. We are never more Christ-like than when we have gone the extra mile with him, immersed ourselves in some degree of his suffering and are enabled, with him, to declare that our lives are complete. Needless to say, that journey to its completion can be a heavy cross to bear.

But it's also necessary to say that from the moment of the Christ's physical death, we are left with no further messianic explanation of the atonement with which to penetrate its mystery. What unfolds in human history, subsequently, are attempts by scholars to explain the cross of Christ. There are four main doctrinal theories of the atonement: the Sacrificial Theory, which has its roots in the scriptural traditions that I have just outlined; the Classic Theory, which, according to the twentieth-century theologian Gustav Aulen (in his seminal work *Christus Victor*), was revived at the Reformation by Martin Luther from the Augustinian tradition; the Judicial Theory, associated with Anselm in the tenth century, which superseded the Classic model with a feudal construct which depended on contemporary cultural notions of "penal substitution", the idea that the Christ paid the price of sin for us; and, finally, the Exemplarist Theory, as propounded by Peter Abelard as a reaction against Anselm at the turn of the eleventh century, and for whom a God who demanded, or indeed needed, a sacrificial "satisfaction" made no sense and for whom the suffering of Christ was purely an exemplar of divine love.

The Sacrificial Theory grew out of the New Testament, specifically Hebrews, and Jewish sin-offerings, which were never meant to be substitutionary, as in seeking the propitiation of God by the killing of a substitute victim. Their significance was rather as an expiation, where the role of a "sinless" victim was representative, not substitutionary.

The Classic Theory has Christ doing battle with and defeating the Devil, the demonic forces that otherwise hold us captive. It was really that simple, as in Mel Gibson's movie.

The Judicial Theory was propounded by Anselm, with his legalistic ideas of "satisfaction", which owed much to the feudalism at the start of the second millennium. Here was the idea of an outraged God conceived as humankind's feudal overlord, who demanded juridical satisfaction. This feudal perception – variously called the Latin or Roman doctrine – has left its mark down the centuries, living on not just in the formal liturgy (witness the *Book of Common Prayer*'s "full, perfect and sufficient sacrifice, oblation and satisfaction for the sins of the whole world") but even in the stiff, imperial language of Victorian hymns and their modern equivalents, with their monarchical ideas of lordly grace and kingship.

The Exemplarist Theory of Abelard started from the position of intent to sin, as in separation from God, on the part of humankind, and offered Christ as the supreme symbol or exemplar of forgiveness, revealing the limitless love of God. This model liberates God from his sin–justice ledger, or judicial bench, in that it simply offers forgiveness in exchange for repentance, with no strings attached. The only condition of grace is that we turn to Christ.

I go into this degree of detail only in order to demonstrate the amount of scholarship and intellectual effort down the ages that has gone into trying to discern why Jesus Christ had to suffer and to die as he did. Because if we have some conception of the answers to those questions, it might provide us with some insight into why we might be asked to suffer and to die, if we are to be disciples of the one who showed us the way. Here it might be helpful to turn to the contemporary German Protestant theologian, Jurgen Moltmann, whose work gave considerable prominence to the question of why a benevolent God should invite us to suffer, as the Christ had suffered, in the face of the evil, disease and brokenness of the world. In his *Theology of Hope* (1964), he suggests that innocent and involuntary suffering cannot be explained as part of the divine order, as if it contributed in some way to God's purpose. Rather, what it does is demonstrate that the love of God overcomes evil and suffering. And there is, therefore, an injunction for Christians to overcome suffering (and that of course includes advances in palliative medicine) as a means of demonstrating faith in the strength of that divine partnership in this world. It is, if you like, the way in which God appears in the world, through his ability to turn the broken human condition into something new and wonderful – and we must give him the opportunity to do so.

Then, in his *The Crucified God* (1972), Moltmann added the concept of God's solidarity with the world in its suffering. In this work, he speaks of "the godless and the godforsaken", differentiating between those who turn away from or deny the existence of God and the victims of apparently pointless suffering and evil. As the scholar Richard Bauckham puts it: "This is the plight of the world, in the absence of divine righteousness, with which Jesus was identified on the cross."[8] Moltmann was asking: How does God's love reach the godless and the godforsaken? His answer is that it is through God's identification with them through the Christ of the cross. Again, we see the efficacy of a dying Christ who cries to a God who has apparently forsaken him at the moment of his most violent suffering. Again, Bauckham: "This is love which meets the involuntary suffering of the godforsaken with another kind of suffering: voluntary fellow-suffering."[9]

What this introduces is the notion that the cross is necessary in order to bring human experience within the experience of God. As

Bauckham goes on to explain, the cross and God's redemption of it through the resurrection are means through which a broken world that doesn't correspond to a divine perfection, and the new creation in which he does operate, are brought together in the atonement: "His love is such that it embraces the godforsaken reality that doesn't correspond to him, and so he suffers."[10] In doing so, he overcomes the contradiction between the two states and delivers from sin, suffering and death. It's the cry of desolation of Jesus from the cross which brings God into our suffering and makes it redemptive and salvific: "The love between them now spans the gulf which separates the godless and the godforsaken from God and overcomes it."[11]

This is a radical reinterpretation of the role of the atonement and one that is a long way from a simple sacrificial substitution – indeed, if the Christ died to end our suffering, then how come we still suffer? The answer is that the cross does not solve the problem of suffering, but offers a means through which God can share solidarity in our suffering, just as in their godly way the women at the cross show their solidarity with the Christ when the men have run away. Jesus may not have known in Gethsemane that this was the plan, but it is implicit in the decision of faith to go through with it, rather than have the cup pass him by, because "Thy will be done." In this idea, God doesn't intend us to abolish suffering through faith, but does offer a promise to abolish what Moltmann calls "the suffering in suffering". As Bauckham observes, this does not, furthermore, promise a fatalistic submission to the inevitability of suffering, but does argue strongly for a discipleship of ours that demonstrates solidarity with those who suffer, through the demonstration of fellow-suffering love to those in need – the poor, the sick, the suffering and the dying.

And that presupposes that the terminally ill, the suffering and the dying, far from being burdens on us or victims who are to be released prematurely from their suffering, are gifts to us through whom the solidarity of the fellow-suffering of divine love, reflected in human love, can be demonstrated. The example Christians have been shown is not one in which the disciples "assisted Jesus to die" in Gethsemane so that he might avoid his fate, but one in which they failed to show the kind of loving solidarity with him which God would so effectively demonstrate. It follows that we are not being compassionate in dispatching from this life those who are close to death, but should rather be demonstrating a godly and loving solidarity with them by ensuring that their last days and hours are as comfortable and pain-free as humanly possible, which is what the British palliative medical profession has achieved in recent decades and which euthanasia threatens to usurp, until such time as God can show his final and miraculous solidarity with them.

Notes

1. *On the Trinity*, 5.2–3.
2. In *Divine Foreknowledge, Four Views*, Paternoster, 2001.
3. Gregory Boyd, *God of the Possible*, Baker, 2000.
4. In *Beyond the Bounds*, Crossway, 2003.
5. Jurgen Moltmann, *The Crucified God*, SCM, 1974.
6. *Process Theology – an Introductory Exposition*, Cobb and Griffin, Westminster, 1976..
7. Sallie McFague, *Metaphorical Theology*, Fortress, 1982.
8. David F Ford ed., *The Modern Theologians*, Blackwell, 2000.
9. Ibid.
10. Ibid.
11. Ibid.

CHAPTER 6

LAST WORDS

So much for background theology. But abstract theologies of theodicy (the latter being an understanding of why God allows suffering) and of the Passion and atonement are of little use to us unless they have some practical application in the world in which we live. Our scriptures chronicle the struggle of the ancients to make meaning of human life and to understand the mind of God, and the church and philosophical theology have delivered the same task to contemporary generations. There is no practical point beyond the intellectual, fruitful as the exercise might be, in deepening an understanding as to why God allows human suffering, or why the Christ suffered and died, unless we can understand the meaning of these things in the context of our own lives and deaths. So how can our theology relate to our morality on the issue of euthanasia?

For some, the Christian tradition of critical thinking opens the door to assisted suicide and euthanasia. Paul Badham, whose family experience I referred to in the Introduction to this book, is Professor of Theology and Religious Studies in the University of Wales, Lampeter, and is an Anglican priest, as I am. He has written a book, flagged as "Voluntary euthanasia reassessed", with the title *Is There a Christian Case for Assisted Dying?* To which question he replies with a resounding "Yes". It is a good, persuasive and thoughtful book, which arrives at widely different conclusions from mine, but which is evidently steeped in the author's compassion. Professor Badham's exegesis is formed of his own experience, and he is as entitled to interpret his theology in the context of his own worldview as any of the rest of us, if we are to adopt a contextual theology.

In this regard, it is dangerous and potentially patronizing to paraphrase any scholar's work. But I have to try to encapsulate a theme. Much of Professor Badham's thesis comprises the notion that God longs for us to be with him in his eternity and hates us to suffer, so it is entirely rational to kill oneself when terminally ill, or indeed to assist someone who is, as that satisfies God's will. As a contribution to a progressive theodicy, that seems to me to be somewhat limited and limiting.

For instance, Badham argues that the "essential difference" between a Christian and secular worldview is that, from a secular viewpoint, this world is all there is and death marks the end of our existence. "By contrast," he writes, "from a Christian perspective death is the gateway to eternal life." He continues:

> This should have a profound effect on the way we
> approach the dying process. If death is not the final
> terminus, but a junction point from which we move on
> to a new and fuller life with God, then this calls into
> question the desirability of straining to keep this mortal
> life in being if it has become an existence characterised by
> unbearable suffering with no realistic expectation of relief
> or recovery.[1]

He invokes the radical Roman Catholic theologian Hans Küng in support of this position:

> Those who trust in God at the same time trust that death
> is not the end. In the light of the Eternal One, who alone
> can grant "deep deep eternity", the death of mortal life
> becomes transcended into God's eternal life... So should
> I be anxiously concerned how short or long this life is
> finally to be?[2]

Badham takes Küng's argument further, arguing strongly that

> if one believes in a life beyond, then when death comes in
> the fullness of time it should be embraced and accepted,
> or even, as Hans Küng argues, deliberately chosen, if
> the alternative is simply prolongation of this life "under
> conditions which are no longer commensurate with
> human dignity".[3]

This seems to me to be profoundly wrong, for a number of reasons. Note, for one thing, that he says "when death comes *in the fullness of time*", yet this statement ignores that assisted suicide and euthanasia place human limitations on the length and fullness of our time in this world. No one could argue with death being embraced when it comes – how else to explain the Christ's words from the cross in John's Gospel, "It is finished", or in Luke's account, "Father, into your arms I commend my spirit"? But Badham and Küng appear stuck in a kind of classical theistic mindset, with a transcendent and impassible God waiting "on the other side" to greet us into a kind of eternal, heavenly theme-park. They take no account of an open or process theism (discussed in Chapter Five), which not only endeavours to put God into his creation in the incarnation, but which also begins to make sense of Christ's atonement, without which there could be no resurrection, and a Passion through which God redeems both us and him. For we can't rise with him on Easter Sunday unless we've died with him on Good Friday. To die "with him" on Wednesday or Thursday seems to me to be rather missing the point. To follow the Küng/Badham line to its ineluctable conclusion, we might as well throw the towel in earlier in life as and when we feel like joining God in his eternity; Badham is careful to say throughout his book that he is only claiming a Christian case for "assisted dying" and euthanasia (the distinction between these two acts isn't always clear) for the terminally ill who are close to death, but the effect of his common cause with Küng is to make a case for suicide as a sacrament, whether he intends to do so or not.

In the examination of theism and eschatology in Chapter Five, we examined the idea that the Kingdom of Heaven is not some parallel universe that we enter when we die, but rather is to be built by us, with God's help, here in this life and this world – indeed, Jesus teaches that it is "among us" and "within us". In this context, an opt-out function is absurd. A Christian Aid advertising campaign adopted the catchphrase "We believe in life before death". I always thought Christian Aid sailed dangerously close to a secularist wind there, but its theological provenance is nonetheless sound. God wants his creation to live – and in the imperfection of our lives there is a divine will and purpose, even in the worst places, even in the "pit of Sheol", as the Psalm has it, because it is there, as at the cross, that he reaches into human life as it meets death, when we, with him, can truly say, "It is finished."

Indignity in dying

Like all apologists for euthanasia, Küng is also big on human dignity at the point of death. Those who take relatives and friends to die at (note the name) Dignitas invariably speak of wanting those they accompany "to die with dignity". The UK euthanasia lobby organization, Dignity in Dying, needs no further introduction. The driving imperative behind those who believe we should choose our deaths like our holiday destinations is that we should have "dignified" exits. I think I know what they mean: Peaceful and gentle deaths, with control over the event of death, in the manner that they enjoyed autonomy and control, so far as they could, over the events of their lives. Whether this is "dignity" or not is a moot point; it may also involve elements of pride and hubris, to which I will return.

The autonomy of individualism and our consumerist age's obsession with choice (the roots of which were traced in Chapter One) clearly play their role. In Professor Badham's book, he comes back to his father's terrible struggle with death, with which he opens the book, when he seeks to make some theological sense of it:

> A priest of his generation and his belief system would
> not have chosen an assisted death, even if it had been
> available. But I cannot help but think that it would have
> been so much better for him if both the law of the land
> and the teaching of the Church could have enabled him to
> lay down his life with dignity at the time of his choosing.[4]

There in that final line appear the post-modern totems of dignity and choice again. It's revealing that Badham concedes that a previous generation would have interpreted their faith – though note that Badham, an Anglican priest, artfully avoids the word in favour of the altogether more dismissive "belief system" – through a profound and intuitive theodicy, witnessing to a gospel truth that their lives were not their own, to be disposed of as they pleased. I'm afraid that there is a sub-text here; Badham may be implying that this previous generation was foolish or old-fashioned to hold such opinions. In turn, it suggests that they would have seen things our way if they had just been party to our post-modern sophistications. The suggestion is that if they had known the truth that has been vouchsafed to our generation alone, they would have imbibed a lethal draught when the going got rough and been done with it. But I struggle to see how that would have been more dignified than their own stoicism.

Dignity worries me in this context. It worries me in the sense that God evidently doesn't go in for dignity. The atonement that we discussed in Chapter 5 shows us a Christ who chooses the indignity of death (chooses, because he could have escaped this fate); as Paul puts it, he humbled himself "to take the form of a servant" and to be obedient to death, "even death upon a cross". It hardly needs restating, but this amounts to being tortured to death, naked in the midday heat, losing control of bodily functions, despairing at having been forsaken by God. Not much "dignity" there. Unless, of course, you believe that those final words, "It is finished", change everything, forever, as this utter submission to the humility of death is redeemed by God into something he, rather than we, makes glorious.

My father died after some six years in a nursing home, after a series of progressive strokes that left him immobile and, frustratingly, barely able to speak, though his mind was all there until the end. Like Professor Badham with his father, I imagine, I longed for him to die and often wished that he would. This was no life for a bright, formerly fit and articulate man, who had taken pride in a military bearing and a sharp turn of phrase. I didn't get down from London to see him in Somerset as often as I should have done and I regret that now. In his final days, I found myself feeding him his lunch with a spoon and, as he lay dying, I read to him a bit, as one would read a child a bedtime story.

Had anyone told me in advance that this would happen to us, let alone if we had envisaged it a decade or so previously, I'm sure I would have found the prospect as abhorrent and depressing as Dad would have done. I would have anticipated it as an act of humiliation, a literally pathetic circumstance in which the natural order had been overturned and my father's dignity expunged from his character. In the event, it was a transcendental moment that – and I do believe I can speak for him – we both cherished. I look back on it with great affection and, however it is mysteriously worked, I expect he does too. I was offered an opportunity to exercise a sacramental servant ministry for someone I loved more than I had previously appreciated – and without these final acts of care I wouldn't have had the chance to appreciate the depth of that love. The story had turned full circle; the one who had once held me on his knee, had fed and clothed me (and that had been a struggle for him), was for a very short while entirely dependent on my care and comfort. Here was no embarrassment, no awareness of incapacity or dependence, just an acceptance this was a time for me to feed and read and for him to eat and listen. He had told me stories when I was small and now this was his turn, and I was part of it and happy to be so. And he was happy too.

The predictable and entirely reasonable response to this is that I was fortunate, indeed richly blessed, to have a father, at a great age, dying in reasonable comfort, still able to eat and drink, albeit with that assistance. It is characteristic for those who support the introduction of "assisted dying" to claim, in many cases sincerely, that they are only proposing such actions for people who are both terminally ill (some limit their proposals to those for whom death is "imminent") and in unbearable pain. I gather from Professor Badham's story that his own father fell into one of these categories; he was suffering greatly, I understand, and I cannot imagine how differently I would have felt towards my father's end were he in a dark despair of agony (though the event of my mother's death, described in the Introduction to this book, perhaps offers me some insight).

But the point is not to be made so glibly that those who can and wish to die as my father did, relatively comfortably and peacefully, should do so and good luck to them. Meanwhile, those who are not so blessed should apparently have the capacity to take the only peaceful initiative available to them, a pharmaceutically engineered end. Because these deaths – the peaceful and the agonizing – are not separate and unrelated. They are linked, as all humankind is linked, in the manner that John Donne described: "Every man's death diminishes me". If it were otherwise, then we would not wish for everyone to enjoy the kind of end that my father had.

The answer, to which we must aspire, is that we must direct our intent, our resources, our efforts and our money at ensuring that everyone can have the sort of death my father had, or better, and that no one has to suffer the pain and agony, and their attendant despair and humiliation, of the kind of deaths we all despise and fear, irrespective of whether or not we're in favour of euthanasia. The way to achieve that utopian ideal is through ever-improving standards of palliative care. That is not pie in the sky, it is achievable, as Chapter Four on end-of-life care tried to demonstrate. But it is less likely that we will achieve a world in which standards of palliative care are sufficiently high to ensure that no one need die in the "unbearable pain" that euthanasia enthusiasts use as leverage for its legislative introduction. If we are offering death as a clinical "treatment", then we are always accepting that there will be circumstances that our terminally ill people find intolerable and from which death is the only rescue. As we have seen, the nature of palliative care also changes once death is a clinical option – in many respects, we would be perpetuating suffering by putting euthanasia and assisted suicide on the statute book.

We are, in other words, accepting defeat once we formalize death as the only way out of physical suffering. The alternative – and, as Professor Badham acknowledges, previous generations knew that faith offered this alternative – is that we continue to battle for a world in which all deaths are something like my father's and none are like his father's. That can only happen if we don't give in to death by accepting it as a medical option. It is to be managed, not to be promoted. We can have a world in which all natural death can be comfortable. We should aspire to that. And that really would be dignified.

A slippery slope?

It is often said that a risk contingent on the introduction of a limited degree of assisted suicide is that it would open a "slippery slope" to euthanasia. While there may be an essential truth behind the sentiment, it's not an entirely satisfactory metaphor. It suggests that legislation for limited application of the practice – for example, for the introduction of assisted suicide for terminally ill adults in unbearable pain – could be an act that generates unintended consequences. But it is clear that, for many in the "assisted dying" lobby, these consequences would be far from unintended. The lobby group Dignity in Dying changed its name from the Voluntary Euthanasia Society as recently as 2006. The Society was founded in 1931 and the executive of its new manifestation is accustomed to referring to its long campaigning history, so it continues to claim its heritage in the pro-euthanasia movement. It is difficult to avoid the assumption that the organization is embarked upon a campaign to win euthanasia in the UK by a series of gradual increments, of which the introduction of limited assisted suicide would be the first. This is not so much a slippery slope of unintended consequences as a deliberately plotted path down into an abyss whose destination is euthanasia. There is nothing unintended about it; much of the assisted-suicide lobby want what is at the bottom of the slope, and it's a slow and deliberate climb down into that dark valley.

There was resistance to the lobby's name change at the time, by those parts of the medical profession that recognized the strategy being undertaken for what it is. The Association of Palliative Medicine and the Medical Ethics Alliance wrote to the government at the start of 2006 to urge it to reject the euthanasia charity's application for a new trademark based on the phrase "dignity in dying":

> Dignity in dying is a phrase in common parlance in many sections of the population, being used by patients worried about the care they will receive. Patients often ask whether they will have dignity in dying because they are frightened, feel abandoned, are worried they might be left incontinent, confused or in another state that will undermine their personal dignity. These patients are not asking for euthanasia or assisted suicide; they are asking for good care. For the Voluntary Euthanasia Society to seek a monopoly of a common English phrase in order to invest it with a totally different meaning is dishonest and will create confusion.

Another strategy of the pro-euthanasia movement is to deploy a contrived appeal to democracy, suggesting that a referendum of the British people would reveal majority support for assisted suicide. This line demonstrates a tenuous grasp of democracy. A majority of the British population supports the re-introduction of capital punishment, but Dignity in Dying unsurprisingly does not include a "Bring Back Hanging" clause in its manifesto. Elected representatives are mandated to govern and have consistently rejected proposed legislation for assisted suicide. This is partly why the pro-euthanasia lobby switched from the proper tactic of endeavouring to achieve its aims through the legislature to winning direction from a cabal of sympathetic Law Lords to have the Director of Public Prosecutions "clarify" when a person assisting a suicide would not be prosecuted under the Suicide Act 1961, shifting the DPP's role from one in which he is the cold and objective assessor of the public interest in prosecution to one of arbitration between supposedly good and bad motives for suicide assistance.

The abortion axis

Another area of medical ethics regularly raised in the euthanasia debate is the precedent of abortion. There is a particularly vigorous Catholic lobby, which seeks to equate some aspects of end-of-life care with our attitudes to abortion. It is argued that where there is resistance to the taking of human life for the terminally ill, there is relatively little equivalent protection for the lives of unborn babies. Appealing as it is, there is an inherent weakness in this argument in that, however passionately it might be held in some quarters that human life begins at the moment of conception, there are alternative arguments with regard to when foetal life is both viable and valid. Were it not so, there would not be the periodic arguments, in Parliament and elsewhere, over the time limits at which abortions can legally be conducted. No such equivocation can exist with assisted suicide, since the human life at stake is self-evidently extant, with all the rights and sanctities that attach to that life. Attempts to establish a moral equivalence between assisted suicide and abortion, as a kind of pro-life campaign at both ends of human existence, also enable the pro-euthanasia lobby to claim that resistance to its aims arises solely from dogmatic religious sources – the pro-life, anti-abortion movement being primarily associated with Roman Catholic doctrine. While clearly there are objections to assisted suicide and euthanasia rooted in theology, the range of resistance is far wider than the principally religious objections to abortion.

Where there is a resonance between the oppositions to euthanasia and to abortion is in perceived threats to society's most vulnerable. For a pro-life campaigner, there can be nothing more vulnerable than the unborn child. For the anti-euthanasia campaigner, the recognized threat is not only to the vulnerable – the terminally sick, the elderly, those who fear that they may be becoming a burden – but also to those who can be made vulnerable by the existence of a law that moves into the public sphere the notion that the deliberate taking of life can be interpreted as a clinical methodology and a valid "lifestyle choice". Once the deliberate taking of human life is approved by the state, then the option to exercise that right is ever-present, like a dark presence. Indeed, it brings an entirely new and sinister meaning to the funeral liturgy: "In the midst of life we are in death." That has, in ecclesiological terms, always stood as a testament to the constant presence of our mortality in our earthly lives. In a world with euthanasia, it becomes a statement of our intent in relation to that mortality. Suddenly, mortality doesn't attend us, but we can attend to our mortality when we wish. The words are no longer a celebration of life in its eternal proximity to death, but an acknowledgment of the triumph of death as it has entered our lives as a simple consumer choice.

Our relationship with this ever-present mortality relates to our compassion, literally our capacity for "suffering with" those who are close to death and, indeed, in respect of our **own sufferance of death**. It is a human replication of our understanding, through the theodicy that we discussed in Chapter Five, of the manner in which our God suffers with us. It follows that every suicide is a failure to have honoured the intimate relationship between life and death. The death is only truly tragic if its inevitability has been acknowledged by the hastening of it – the Shakespearian question, "Death where is thy sting?" has been answered by the suicide with the surrender and supplication that it is right here, right now. True compassion is to be found in the acknowledgment of death's inevitability but, in contrast to hastening it, a defiance of it is to defeat it with the honouring of life until the moment of its natural end. Life becomes the celebratory constant, rather than the death that interrupts it. And it's in the affirmation of life that we cope with death. The Church of England addressed this very theme in its response submission to the DPP's interim policy for prosecutors on assisted suicide in 2009:

> The Church of England believes that every suicide is a tragedy and that a caring society ought to ensure that anyone considering suicide is able to have ready access to life-affirming and life-enhancing support, counseling and medical and nursing care. We also recognize that, for a variety of reasons, some people find the thought of continuing their lives so bleak that they choose suicide, sometimes requesting others to assist them in this endeavour. We wish to respond to such people with compassion and empathy but we believe that compassion is best expressed by making every effort to dissuade them from committing suicide, not by assisting them... It is essential... in order to protect human life and, particularly, the lives of vulnerable people, that assisted suicide is never deemed to be acceptable or commendable.[5]

The conclusion must be that assisting a suicide is never compassionate, or at best is a corruption of compassion. It is moral cowardice not so much on the part of the person taking their own life, but on the part of the person who helps them. As Arthur Miller put it in *Death of a Salesman*: "A suicide kills two people."

Life for the living

It has become a commonplace for those who want to put a positive spin on people taking their own lives to claim that they are "forced" to go abroad to do so. A moment's examination demonstrates that no one is forced to take their own lives, without the person or persons doing the forcing almost certainly facing up to fourteen years' imprisonment under the Suicide Act 1961. The rejoinder to this observation tends to reflect the *zeitgeist* of our consumerist culture. The person seeking an assisted suicide is "forced" to go abroad for it, because the object of their desire is not available in Britain. There is no acknowledgment of any imperative beyond an obeisance to "desire", as if it is taken for granted that what we desire is what we should have.

One cannot look in from the outside at the cases of those who have travelled from the UK to Dignitas in Switzerland and presume to understand or to criticize the actions of those who have taken part. But one is entitled to look at the facts. Let's take an example which raises profound issues concerning the right to life and death.

In July 2009, Sir Edward Downes, one of Britain's most respected conductors, travelled to Dignitas with his wife, where both took their own lives in a suicide pact. Sir Edward, eighty-five, had become virtually blind and was losing his hearing, a particularly bitter blow for such a gifted musician. Lady Downes, seventy-four, a former ballet dancer and choreographer, was suffering from cancer. It is not entirely clear whether Lady Downes' condition was terminal. Her condition was clearly not in its terminal stage, but that is very often a significant criterion for those travelling to Switzerland, who want to do so while they are still able. Lady Downes was reported by her family to be concerned about growing too ill to travel, when she deemed the time would have been right to seek an assisted suicide (a principal criticism of the current state of the law among euthanasia supporters). In any event, it would be inappropriate to speculate further in respect of the health of Lady Downes. It is, however, entirely appropriate to consider the implications of Sir Edward's decision to die. His conditions were palpably not life-threatening. His decision was predicated entirely upon his wish to accompany his life partner, to whom he was evidently devoted to the end.

They were accompanied to Dignitas by their grown-up children, Caractacus, forty-one, and Boudicca, thirty-nine. Their son reported:

It was very calm and very simple. The actual final draught is a small glass of clear liquid. They both drank that and laid down on the bed and were both asleep in a couple of minutes. It was very sad but we were content that they had been given the opportunity to end their lives in the way they wanted to.[6]

This is an important act of first-hand witness of the assisted-suicide process and it raises a number of questions. The first, again, relates to the nature of the much-vaunted "dignity" of these occasions. Anyone who has watched deaths will know that they can be sublimely peaceful, even beautiful. They can also be ugly and distressing. We need to decide where on the scale between these two kinds of death the act of self-destruction lies. There will be those who, with Caractacus Downes, find it brave and moving. There will be others who find it distressing and deeply unedifying. The beauty of the moment is only skin-deep – we need to know what really is being done: A human life is being extinguished as a convenience, death by appointment.

But there is a further factor to be taken into account, that is wider than the Downes family's circumstances. It may well be that the two children found the event of their parents' joint suicide profoundly moving, inspiringly peaceful or entirely fulfilling. Or all of these things and more. But it doesn't alter the truth that we are entering a world in which we believe that it may be appropriate for children to watch the suicides of their own parents. And that is a factor that has the potency to change the way in which we think about death, shifting the emphasis significantly from something that happens to us, to something we precipitate, something we choose, a routine option.

We have to start considering who these acts best serve. Clearly, the rationale is that it is the person doing the dying who is benefiting, through release from the life that they can no longer tolerate, or from a future that they fear. But the key question here is this: What does it say about the life that is bequeathed to those who are loved and left behind? For every Caractacus or Boudicca, is there not another child devastated by their parent's premature passing? How sure can parents be that their children truly accepted their choice?

There is a strong temptation to identify something touchingly romantic in a joint suicide of two people who have committed their lives to one another and wish to share their final passage from this life together. One can only watch in awe as two people decline to be parted even in death. It is undeniably an affirmation of great love. But, again, what of those they leave behind? Are we not likely to ponder on the value they might place on the presence of their lives in ours? I might say that I understand why my father might want to take his leave with my mother, but why would he want that more than to stay with me, to share our grief at her loss and to be a memorial to her love for us both? It is, at the very least, an uncomfortable prospect to bear witness to or to assist in the death of a loved one, who would rather go with a greater love, than celebrate that love with the living in whatever time is left of this life.

A time to live

In this book, I have endeavoured to show where the demand for institutionalized assisted suicide and euthanasia has come from. In this respect, it's a heady mix of individualism, consumerism and personal autonomy, all of which threatens to form a new culture for us, replacing ancient notions of our lives lived outwards, with and for other people, those we love. I have traced that process in our society, our politics, our law, our health service and in our established religion. I have looked at actions and outcomes; from the testaments of those who, in despair, have been sorely tempted by suicide but who have won through to renewed hope, a kind of resurrection, to the bitter harvests that are reaped in jurisdictions from Oregon to Switzerland, wherever the despair of euthanasia is sown.

We stand on the threshold of this new millennium with everything to play for. Advances in science, our understanding of the human genome and our opportunity to play God by engineering genetically are growing exponentially; we can push the human lifespan out into the hundreds of years into the broad, sunlit uplands of a disease-free and, God willing, peaceful coexistence. Or we may destroy our planet with carbonized fossil fuels and kill our burgeoning peoples with insufficient resources, a biblical famine of food and water, and wars of ideology and covetousness.

It's as if we stand in awe before a Promised Land, as Moses and his people did. We can embrace it and cultivate it, so it flows with milk and honey. Or we can squander it, crushing the gift of it from previous generations in the maw of our greed and wantonness. When Moses preached to Israel after forty years in the wilderness, he offered the people a choice between the light and dark, between life and death, between the human way and the way of God. He said: "I call heaven and earth to witness against you today that I have set before you life and death, blessings and curses. Choose life so that you and your descendants may live" (Deuteronomy 30:19).

We are offered a similar choice between the sacred and the profane, between divinity and idolatry. We have big choices to make, literally life-or-death decisions. Wherever we encounter it and however challenging it proves to endure, we must choose life, as Moses did. Where we let death in as an optional extra, where we fail to rage against the dark, as we do whenever we start to kill the weakest and least among us, we commit an act of idolatry. Let's choose life, in all that we do, so that we and our descendants may live.

In another book of the Hebrew Bible, the phlegmatic author of Ecclesiastes tells us that "For everything there is a season, and a time for every matter under heaven: a time to be born, and a time to die" (Ecclesiastes 3:1, 2). We are embarking on a season in which momentous decisions will be made with regard to how we live and die. For all of us there will be a time to die. But, in our idolatrous desire for self-determination in this new millennium, let's remember with Charlotte Raven that suicide is rhetoric, life is life, and that in defiance of counsels of despair, we have a time to live.

Notes

1. Paul Badham, *Is there a Christian Case for Assisted Dying?*, SPCK, 2009.
2. *A Dignified Dying: A Plea for Personal Responsibility* (with Walter Jens), SCM, 1995.
3. Badham, *Is there a Christian Case for Assisted Dying?*
4. Ibid.
5. Submission by the Church of England to the Director of Public Prosecutions, 2009.
6. Christopher Hope, *Daily Telegraph*, 14 November 2009.

If you have been or are currently affected by issues in this book...

...you may want to explore further, or seek help and support. Both Care Not Killing and Dying Well, an all-party parliamentary group, have excellent websites:

http://www.carenotkilling.org.uk
http://www.dyingwell.org.uk/

Those seeking further information about palliative care and hospices might like to visit the website of Help The Hospices:

http://www.helpthehospices.org.uk/our-services/information-service/

Samaritans, of course, provides the principal, confidential and non-judgmental support for those considering suicide. The 24-hour UK telephone number is: 08457 90 90 90
Or: http://www.samaritans.org/

In hospital or hospice, doctors and nurses will invariably find time to discuss fears and worries about dying. For spiritual support, ask for access to a chaplain – you don't need to have a religious faith; a chaplain will counsel patients of all faiths and none, or help you to find someone who you may feel more comfortable talking to. The most important thing is to take the first step of talking to someone – there is always help available.

INDEX